BY *Germaine Tillion*

FRANCE AND ALGERIA:
Complementary Enemies (1961)

ALGERIA: *The Realities* (1959)

FRANCE

AND

ALGERIA

Complementary Enemies

GERMAINE TILLION

Translated from the French by

RICHARD HOWARD

GREENWOOD PRESS, PUBLISHERS
WESTPORT, CONNECTICUT

FRANCE
AND
ALGERIA

Complementary

Enemies

Library of Congress Cataloging in Publication Data
Tillion, Germaine.
    France and Algeria.

    Translation of Les ennemis complémentaires.
    Reprint of the ed. published by Knopf, New York.
    1. Algeria--History--1945-1962. I. Title.
[DT295.T5313 1976]   965'.04   76-7572
ISBN 0-8371-8859-8

Originally published in French
as *Les Ennemis complémentaires.*
© 1960 by Les Editions de Minuit.

Originally published in 1961 by Alfred A. Knopf, New York

Reprinted with the permission of Alfred A. Knopf, Inc.

Reprinted in 1976 by Greenwood Press,
a division of Williamhouse-Regency Inc.

Library of Congress Catalog Card Number 76-7572

ISBN 0-8371-8859-8

Printed in the United States of America

CONTENTS

PART 1

1957

I

Complementary Enemies[1]

My 1956 analysis of the Algerian tragedy[2] may have suggested that I considered purely economic measures sufficient to cure the great bleeding ulcer Algeria has become. This misunderstanding explains, I fear, much of the approval my work received.

The effectiveness of exclusively political medication seems quite as chimerical, however, and I regard the Algerian complex as a total phenomenon in which everything will become insoluble if everything is not solved, a double requirement that accounts for the situation's apparently hopeless character. Yet it is France and France alone, to the exclusion of any other

---

[1] This article includes the most important passages of a letter I wrote to Raymond Aron on November 7, 1957. It was published, at the request of Jean Bloch-Michel, in the May 1958 number of the magazine *Preuves*.

[2] Revised six months later and published in 1957 by Les Editions de Minuit. Reprinted by the same publisher in 1960 with other texts under the general title *L'Afrique bascule vers l'avenir*.

nation, which can provide economic remedies, since these remedies relate more to wages as a whole[3] than to the total of investments. Political medication, on the contrary, is henceforth completely out of our hands, and it is increasingly dangerous for France to retain any illusions on this point.

Thus each of the belligerents possesses half of the "miracle drug" that could save this country. As a result, the disease is probably fatal, since the years go by without even the ghost of an agreement in sight.

Frenchmen and Algerians—it is impossible to conceive of two populations whose mutual dependence is

---

[3] At present, there are between 350,000 and 400,000 Algerian workers in metropolitan France, and they support, directly or indirectly, a third of the rural Moslem population in Algeria. French capital invested in Algeria produces wages for slightly over 100,000 workers. On the assumption that this capital is not removed, 1,500 billion (old francs) must be invested in order to repatriate the Algerians who work in France and assure them corresponding wages at home (this on an average basis of 4 million francs' investment for one worker's wages). Moreover, this is a purely academic speculation, for in the near future no nation in the world can invest 1,500 billion francs in Algeria. Further, these 1,500 billion francs would be insufficient to give the Algerians now working in France the equivalent of what they earn there. The Algerians are distributed throughout a labor force in which highly skilled technicians are numerous. Naturally, these technicians must also be imported into Algeria and paid accordingly, which would diminish the total wages distributed to native workers, in a proportion which it is difficult to specify but which is enormous.

more certain. We are bound to them, and they to us, for we can deprive them of all they desire, while they can critically endanger all we aspire to. Neither side has the means to protect itself against attack, though each has a thousand means to inflict it. On each side, women and terrified children are the first to be fired on. Nothing can restrain the terrible inventions of the combatants—not public protest, frontiers, Maginot Line, not even an appeal to some national or international law—for if this is not peace, it is not yet war.

What have they to lose in losing our friendship? Virtually everything, and their wages first of all—that is, their bread, their life, their children's future, and even that freedom paid for at so high a cost. Not to mention friendship.

And what have we lost in losing their trust? Our economic expansion (linked to our Saharan pros-

---

France, on the contrary, which at present lodges some two million foreigners on her soil (60 per cent of whom belong to the "active population"), can without special difficulties considerably increase the total wages paid to Algerians.

On the other hand, France must protect the men and women on Algerian soil who have (or claim) French nationality.

We are consequently obliged to contend, on both sides, with a double current of dependence, an "objective interdependence" that does not exist in French relations with Morocco and Tunisia. It gives the present war its desperate ferocity, but if the stage of war can be "transcended," it could then play its normal role, one beneficial to both nations.

pects), the security of our Algerian compatriots, all our African hopes—in other words, all our goals. Not to mention trust.

A *defeat tied to a victory*

Hence inevitable defeat is attached to the victory each of the two nations seeks to wrench from its adversary. Yet each of these deadly victories is more accessible than the rational peace that could still save everything.

Unlikely on the military level, a French capitulation becomes plausible from a financial point of view. It would represent in theoretical terms an incredible success for the Algerian rebels, but none of their hopes has the slightest chance of surviving this success, for no amount of foreign aid will permit them to support more than a third of their population from one day to the next. At present this population is supported by wages sent from France, and it is lunacy to suppose (if French public opinion were to admit that France had suffered defeat in Algeria) that North African workers could continue earning their living on French soil.

Of course, their repatriation would pose serious problems for French employers, but such problems can be solved. Italians, Spaniards, Yugoslavs, Hungarians, Poles, ask nothing better than to cross our borders with a work contract (not to mention the hundreds of thousands of Tunisian and Moroccan unemployed). On the other hand, the problems posed by Algerian repatriation admit of no solution on their own soil. Here, there would be inevitable famine, reciprocal massacres, the desperate evacuation of all Europeans and even of those Moslems rich or educated enough to find means of escape—an evacuation accompanied by the inevitable collapse of capital. And for the Algerians who could not escape: economic, social, cultural, biological ruin. Consequently political failure as well, the failure of an independence paid for at too high a price.

The military victory, which seems to be our present goal, also remains likely, on account of the increasing adaptation of our army and the extreme lassitude of the rural Moslem populations. It is no less catastrophic. Catastrophic for the French, and for their allies. Catastrophic now, in the future, in Algeria, outside Algeria.

The old structures break down

During the course of a century's control, the French developed and established certain administrative structures on the conquered territory (mixed communes, *caïds, ouakkafs,* and others). I have witnessed their collapse with my own eyes, a collapse that in less than six months has been total and definitive. Yet they had been conceived by men who knew the country well, in a climate psychologically favorable and—to say the least—at leisure. They have been replaced, since 1955, by necessarily hasty improvisations that soldiers ignorant of the country are now attempting to establish (in what circumstances we know, and with what chances of success we can imagine).

The original old structures of the native society have resisted longer, but they too are in the process of breaking down. Tribal partition, authority of the elders, family organization, the special position of women—all these had already suffered encroachments, but nothing comparable to today's real collapse. I know a number of stern, traditionalist Moslem families in which the daughter of the house has switched from the veil to blue jeans and from the harem to the *maquis*, while her old father wavers between consternation and patriotic pride. Who can conceive of a converse transformation: the heroine in trousers agreeing to resume the white *lhaf* of Algiers or the black *haïk* of Constantine and consenting to express her personality henceforth only in her baking?

Collapse of the administrative framework, explosion of the social and family structure . . . What is left? The clandestine nationalist organizations and our military establishment. *Tête-à-tête*. Alone at last.

For in the darkness of rebellion, all the administrations of a modern state have suddenly begun sprouting all over Algeria. And just as our officers, in spite of themselves, have in a hundred years Arabized Kabylia and the Aurès Mountains (merely by creating roads and ensuring their safety), the *fellaga,* unwillingly and unconsciously, have done more to Gallicize their nation in three years than the French during the entire preceding century. Of course, it is to oppose France that they are utilizing French ideas (freedom, democracy, state-supported schools, equality, and resistance to oppression) and against France that they are imitating her civil and military institutions. It is nonetheless true that what we are now destroying in their country is an image of ourselves, as though to add to the horror of the murder we are committing.

The clandestine structure

By the end of 1956, after two years of war, almost all of Moslem society found itself solidly and effectively supported by a clandestine structure: secret magistrates, arbitrating private disputes throughout the country, had lowered the rate of cases judged by official tribunals (by 30 per cent in Algiers, by 100 per cent in Greater Kabylia); civilian officers, unknown to our administration, registered births and deaths; collectors gathered assessments, taxes, and fines, but also paid pensions and family allowances; usury was forbidden, as was prostitution, rioting, and theft; sumptuary laws regulated holidays, excessive expenditures, and dowries, and during the severe food blockade of Kabylia (which is still being maintained), I was unable to discover any evidence of a black market.

It might be supposed that these invisible structures, a powerful wartime weapon, were set in motion long ago. This is probably not the case; the development of the insurrection seems to me to have proceeded rather as follows:

In a first phase, young men (their average age between twenty-five and thirty-five), determinedly modern, with a wide experience of secrecy (often eight to ten years in the higher echelons), political training, strict discipline, and a perfect knowledge of their milieu, set off the insurrection and constituted its hierarchic armature. During this initial period, the Moslem masses followed events—with favor, curiosity, anxiety, but somewhat from outside. By granting them genuine collective concessions, we might, at this point, have still been able to dissociate them from the insurrection.

In a second phase—after December 1955—the masses allowed themselves to be led by the nationalist organizations, and after February 1956 the movement expanded with incredible speed. At the end of this same year (December 1956) the work was done.

During this second phase, the men in control, the men who act, no longer came only from the revolutionary ranks, isolated from the masses by the secrecy necessary to their action; on the contrary, they represented the entire range of the elite of the Algerian population. From that time, it was futile to suppose we could shield that population from their influence. And repression would inevitably find itself confronted by a homogeneous society which it is impossible to destroy and which it will be impossible to spare.

The French political leaders at this point committed the perhaps irreparable mistake of not realizing the irreversible character of the movement occurring in the silent depths of a nation that no longer had either newspapers or representatives. No doubt, too, they failed to evaluate the extent and the scope of the operation they had assumed the responsibility of launching. In short, around September 1956, the Army received orders to annihilate the politico-military ranks of the insurrection "by every means." The politico-military ranks were, in fact, all the village elders, all the city leaders, all the educated youth. This brings us to the war's third phase.

The French Army in Algeria is a very impressive one: aggressive, effective, well-trained, and incomparably seasoned.

The Army does what it is told without having the right to choose its goals, and for a year and a half[4] it has applied itself, in accordance with the orders it has received, to destroying the original armature of a na-

---

[4] This was written in November 1957.

tion toward which we had such a great responsibility. The Army applies itself not without results, and "by every means." But if it attains its goal (and it is likely to), with what will we replace what it is in the process of destroying?

Our non-commissioned officers overseas are municipal councilors, teachers, agricultural advisers, even midwives—without detriment to their military and police functions. Are they now going to be the paternal authority, the national ideal, the religious example too? Are they going to renounce forever the notion of returning to their own villages in order to perform the roles of this astounding substitution across the sea? Unfortunately, if it is likely that we are destroying the entire vital structure of this nation, it is certain that we shall not replace it, and no less certain that the stubborn, desperate, murderous anarchy (from now on the only patrimony of these wretched peoples) will not be limited to their frontiers and that we ourselves, one fine day, will pay dearly for the chaos we are creating.

The Algerian "Diaspora"

On the African continent—that tremendous iceberg drifting toward unknown seas—there was an active dispersion of Algerians—a "Diaspora"—long before 1954, which was the direct result of our good works and our wrongdoing, always closely combined. By our good works I mean the mass of training and "modern experience" that France put at the disposal of the Algerian people (for we must not forget, to our credit, that the Algerian people are by far the most highly developed in the Arab world). By our wrongdoing I mean the blockade our Algerian compatriots have set up against the invasion of the young Moslem elite, a blockade that forces the young leaders unwilling to be "domestic exiles" to become expatriates.

The Algerian "Diaspora," considerably increased in number and in importance since the spread of the conflict (spring 1956), has gradually rallied to the forces of the F.L.N. (Front de Libération Nationale) and at present plays a disquieting role in the domestic and foreign policies of Tunisia, Morocco, and even French West Africa and the Middle East. If we achieve that military victory which has been promised us for over three years, we must expect to see "Algeria in exile" swell to disproportionate size and adopt an attitude of a chronic hostility. Now, whether we like it or not, it is impregnable and holds, moreover, the means of destroying any likelihood of progress and peace on the African continent, where it can certainly ruin our Saharan hopes.

The French of Algeria

We have thus far discussed only an Algerian Algeria, so to speak. Confronting this Algeria is another, as tenacious, as dangerous, as exposed: French Algeria. To abolish the former for the sake of the latter is not only inhuman—but impossible; to abolish the latter for the sake of the former is just as barbarian—but just as impractical. Does a middle course exist? Yes, to abolish both, by the repatriation of a French minority richest in technicians and money: uproot the French of Algeria and abandon the other Algerians to crushing misery. This last solution is nevertheless not the worst. And certainly not the most likely.

In the forests of the American Northwest live a number of tremendous, stupid, and bellicose bull moose; occasionally two of them entangle their huge antlers and die of hunger, muzzle to muzzle. It is these moose we must remember in measuring the balance of forces confronting each other, for their proportions are as diabolically matched as those of the two beasts.

If the Moslems were less numerous, assimilation would have already been carried out, for it has had numerous supporters among them. If the non-Moslem population of Algeria were less compact and less organized, a solution of the Tunisian type would not offer a serious difficulty, for the native Algerian elite is quite superior to what is generally believed and has in the last three years given proof that it is qualified to lead a nation.

But the numerical balance of the two groups (one against eight) is only an optical illusion, for if strength is in numbers, it is not in numbers alone; investments, technology, populous and organized cities, also figure in a nation's potential. Our Algerian compatriots— concentrated, organized, armed, terrified, aggressive— are certainly the stronger where they have settled, in Algiers, in Oran, in Bône. We cannot let them be massacred; nor can we be certain they will not commit the massacre themselves. In short, indefinite war—declining, from catastrophe to lassitude, to segregations of the Mau Mau type on African soil, to the gradual expulsion of the Algerians on ours—seems to me the most hideous but also the easiest solution. Out of lack of imagination and civic courage, each side is inexorably drifting toward it.

By chance I have before me a paragraph from *L'Echo d'Alger*, dated October 2, 1957; it refers to a gentleman named Marcel living in El-Biar, of whom we are told: "The madman would not listen to reason, and threw a grenade out the window at the police. . . . The lunatic was taken to the Mustafa Hospital." No indication of surprise in the reporter's tone: it is quite natural, if your name is Marcel and you live in El-Biar, to have a grenade in the kitchen drawer and to throw it on a sudden impulse, or when the blood runs to your head, at the representatives of authority. No need to speculate about the difficulties the poor lunatic would have made for himself if his name had been Ali or Mohammed (which, after all, is no guarantee against mental alienation), but let us consider the problems posed by all these Marcels, Jeans, or Roberts, remembering that all of them, from fifteen-year-olds to old men of seventy-five, are armed.

It is true that there are not 1,200,000 of them, as we are told. In fact, we must first agree on a definition of the people we are discussing. What is a Frenchman? And what are the criteria that permit us to define him? Blood group? Patronym? Religion? Electoral College? *Carte d'identité?* Almost anything—or nothing—can characterize this person. I therefore propose a practical definition (though one that requires consulting the people themselves): A Frenchman is someone who considers himself to be French.

In Algeria, who claims this label? Certainly the non-Moslems (there are 1,042,409 of these, including 49,-979 who are non-naturalized); perhaps the dissident Moslems (Mozabites), whose number is uncertain (60,000?) and whose opinions are more uncertain still. (The Mozabites are usually figured in the European majority, though some have rallied to the F.L.N.). In any case and without any doubt, we must include, along with the minority groups, a certain number of

Moslems of the majority. How many? No one knows; all that we know is that some of them want to remain French, to the point of risking their lives to do so; that each "effort" of pacification has massively diminished their number (though the "efforts" of the insurrection have, on the contrary, increased it); and that some still subsist—silent, dismayed—between the two "efforts," between the downstream alluvial deposit and the upstream erosion.

Who would dare contest their title to be French, if they still wanted to be—with a berth on the *Mayflower* of the colonial backwash and the wherewithal to establish themselves like anyone else on our soil? (The legitimate return of the expedition of Charles X.)

To distinguish this man—our indisputable compatriot—from the *felleg* who resembles him like a brother, constitutes, it is true, an arduous exercise, one to which the forces of order have devoted themselves in vain during the last three years. Their failure is excusable, for the interested parties themselves do not always recognize who they are, and every day grow a little more confused.

There are 6,552 Algerians who have consented to appear in the municipal delegations, and 239 others are French officials in the "conception and direction" category. I have many friends in both groups, and I know what burden of bitterness they bear, regardless of their dedication. Somewhere in the heart of these two chosen phalanxes there may be firm supporters of our regime who are not its victims; I myself have never encountered them.

Conversely, our adversaries' most qualified representatives are at present crowded together in camps and prisons, where I visit them when I have the chance (moreover, they are brothers and cousins of those in the former group, and I have known some of them, too, for twenty years). It is possible, even probable, that among them are the hate-filled, narrow-minded fanatics we hear about so often. As far as I know, I have never met such men. Those I know are anxious and agonized, divided between the most contradictory choices, filled with mistrust for what comes from us but still more mistrustful of all that does not come.

To find an immediate formula of association

What about the atrocities?

They are only too real, I know them only too well: I have seen Mélouza, I have examined the publications of the Government-General, I have questioned the pathetic mutilated creatures. It is all true, and horrible, but it is no more representative of the Algerian people than other atrocities (whose dreadful catalogue is also lengthening) are representative of France. I have been informed about them in detail, too, and they make me sick with shame and disappointment. By abstaining from punishing those responsible (which is, unfortunately, what we have done) we deny ourselves the right to judge our enemies.

I am not eager to speak of our crimes, or of those of the Algerians, for we must accept each other, and if we all want to "win" this war, we must find—not in twelve years, as with Germany, and not even tomorrow, but right now—a formula of association that works for both sides.

What will it be? Any at all, provided we can agree on it with our adversaries. For if France agreed to Algerian independence, it would thereby lose most of its disadvantages. Conversely, if the Algerian rebels agreed to the *loi-cadre*, it would be flexible enough to satisfy their needs very quickly. Between independence and the *loi-cadre* exists a whole series of intermediary solutions that would oblige us to make concessions which we are certainly determined to agree to, and which, moreover, we shall not avoid in any case. So why not take the trouble to consider them? Because that would mean recognizing our adversaries' legal existence. Rather continue the war indefinitely. Rather ruin our country without recourse. Rather sacrifice the security of our Algerian compatriots and our Saharan hopes.

The most authentic patrimony a nation can have

is the worth of the men who inhabit it, but they must be given the nourishment they need in order to grow. It is a cruel irony for the Algerian population to accumulate the values and needs of an adult people, a "developed" people, with the material means of a minor nation. This discrepancy between values and means, between needs and possibilities, is obviously one of the elements of the present despair—it will perhaps be the source of tomorrow's catastrophes—but it could also be the wellspring of a surprising progress and thereby of a stable peace. And just as the Algerian war is a cancer that will devour Africa, a true Algerian peace, based on mutual consent, consolidated by real and reciprocal advantages, could gradually regenerate the great African body now a prey to so many sicknesses.

Each of us—our adversaries and ourselves—has half the remedy that can save the Algerian people, so heroic and so wretched. If, out of blind hate, stupidity, or impotence, we abandon each other for the easy solution of war to the death, indefinitely pursued, then woe on us, on them, and on all around us. And yet, in both scales—that of material means (which are ours) and that of the desire for progress (the indisputable patrimony of the rebel youth)—amid the cruel sufferings of these three years, despite these sufferings, because of these sufferings, certain resources have been accumulated.

This is not a metaphysical image. The development of the Algerian people is a fact, and the incredible energy that in the last three years has impelled these people toward the future appears in the entire social life of this nation and even in the ordinary vocabulary of the women still shut up in harems. In the mountain villages, the old men (traditional guides of public opinion) now say: "We are old fools; the young are braver and wiser than we are." As for the young, they dream only of modernism, equality, democracy, secularization—and, naturally, independence, the magic word that contains all the rest.

By a surprising coincidence (in which political machinations have played a minor role) at the same time that these people, so long oppressed and misunderstood, demanded a name, a patrimony, and reasons to live, their half-desert earth revealed its tremendous reserves of energy. But with human values, as with the energy beneath the earth, it is not enough merely for them to exist; they must be acquired. They need a minimum of opportunity in order to bear fruit. Algeria has made an appeal to the future—the most violent, the most impassioned, the most "qualified" of all Africa. A whole continent will be oriented according to our answer.

II

Testimony for a Man Condemned to Death

THIS ACCOUNT *was written in 1957, immediately after the arrest of the persons named in this text (September 24, 1957), in case of my own death.*

Foreseeing various eventualities, I had thirty copies mimeographed and sent to friends I trusted.[1] I knew that they would not exploit these facts politically, but that they could not be kept from speaking if for one reason or another I myself was prevented from offering my testimony.

I also sent a copy to the lawyers who were to defend those concerned: Maître Théo Bernard and Maître Gautherat, of the Paris bar, and Maître Yves Gonon, of the Algiers bar.

It seemed preferable not to let the facts contained

---

[1] In particular, to the president of the bar, Maître Paul Arrighi, and to Jean Bloch-Michel, Albert Camus, Geneviève de Gaulle, and André Postel-Vinay. I also sent copies to the cabinet of M. René Coty, to the keeper of the seals (M. Lecourt), and to several members of the High Court.

in this document be published until the trials had taken place, and I took the necessary precautions.

During the year before and the year after May 13, 1958, official Algeria lived under a special regime, unrelated to either the Fourth or the Fifth French republics. Under this regime, everyone had his say in governing Algiers and a variety of highhanded policies were pursued. This regime, contrary to the estimation of the French Left, does not seem to me to correspond to fascism (which usually has a state and a ruling concept) but can claim the title of authoritarian anarchy.

Either by chance or through the malice of the local synarchs,[2] the dates of Saadi Yacef's three trials were set during the period when the confusion was at its peak: June 24, July 1, and August 25, 1958.

Yacef's lawyers knew that I was prepared to give evidence when and where they wished. They decided I should come to Algiers to take the stand at the second trial (July 3). I did come, and the tribunal immediately declared that the case would be tried in private session.

For the third trial, the lawyers decided not to have me recalled, but instead to read a part of the text given below, which had been in their hands for several months. On this occasion, they communicated its con-

---

[2] Before leaving, I had received threats which I am still uncertain whether to characterize as of the "intimidation" or "warning" type.

*tents to the press. Various newspapers gave résumés
of or extracts from it; the weekly L'Express chose to
publish the entire text.*

I met M. Saadi Yacef and Mlle Zohra Drif on
July 4 and August 9, 1957, but I learned M. Yacef's
name only on the occasion of our second encounter
and that of Mlle Drif only at the moment of her arrest, on September 24, 1957, from the press.

In case I should be prevented from giving evidence,
I wish to state in writing all the facts of which I have
been made directly aware and which relate to these
two meetings.

These meetings were possible only because I had
spent long periods in Algeria for scientific purposes
since 1934 and had made many friendships among the
Moslem population. It is therefore necessary to specify
certain circumstances previous to these meetings in
order to place the facts that follow in their proper
perspective.

From 1934 to 1950 I worked as ethnologist on a
scientific mission in the Aurès, and during these years
I accumulated considerable documentation concerning
the peasant societies of this region. My fourth mission
came to an end on May 30, 1940. I then returned to
Paris. I immediately set up a Resistance group, a
sector of an organization known as the Musée de

l'Homme Hauet-Vildé network. Of the four leaders of this organization (Colonel de la Rochère, Boris Vildé, Colonel Hauet, and myself) I am now the only survivor; the first was shot and the other two died during deportation. I myself was arrested by the Gestapo on August 13, 1942, and my charge included five "justifications" of the death sentence.[3]

After three years' imprisonment, I was repatriated on July 10, 1945, but since most of my scientific documents had been stolen by the German police, I requested the National Center of Scientific Research to transfer me, on a temporary basis, from the Ethnology section to that of Modern History.

In November 1954, Professor Massignon, who had been my thesis adviser, asked me to come with him to speak to the Minister of the Interior, at that time M. Mitterrand. M. Mitterrand assured Professor Massignon that there was no question of bombarding the Aurès with naphtha (as the rumor then had it) and offered to send me there to examine the conditions in which the transfer of certain tribes had been carried out.

I could not, in all conscience, refuse this mission, and I left in December. In the Aurès I was able to observe that if the transfer of the tribes in question

---

[3] My rank is that of commander (officer of the Légion d'honneur; officer of the Resistance; *Croix de guerre avec palme*).

had been quite futile, at least it had been carried out humanely enough.

I then traveled through the various valleys of this region in all directions for three months, and I was dismayed by their economic collapse, whose causes I then began to analyze.

During this period Governor-General Léonard had been replaced by Governor-General Soustelle (whom I had known some twenty years before at the Musée de l'Homme) and it was to him that I presented my report. On this occasion I discussed with him the impoverishment of Algeria and the remedies that could be applied; he asked me to remain in his cabinet as a *chargé de mission*.

From March 1955 to February 1956 I remained in Algiers in this function and studied, in particular, the economic, ethnic, and social data of the Algerian problem, while, of course, following the development of the political problem, though in a less direct way. It was during this period that I proposed to M. Soustelle the creation of a service to be called the Social Centers, a project to which he gave his complete support.

When M. Lacoste replaced M. Soustelle, I postponed my return to France for three months at the latter's request, in order to discuss with the new minister a plan of compulsory education in Algeria and, in the framework of my regular studies, to revisit certain regions of this country.

At the end of 1956 I wrote a brochure that appeared in the first weeks of 1957 and was called *L'Algérie en 1957*,[4] in which I discussed the increasing breakdown of the underdeveloped regions and expressed my conviction that it was absolutely necessary for Algeria to live in economic symbiosis with France. This brochure is at the source of the facts I am discussing—that is, my meetings with Saadi Yacef.

On June 18, 1957, I flew to Algiers with four other members of the International Commission on Internment.

I have been a member of this commission since its origin, and when it decided to investigate conditions in Algeria, I was chosen, along with M. Martin-Chauffier, to accompany our three colleagues from abroad. It was in these circumstances that I visited the principal camps and prisons of Algeria.

During this trip, I again met many friends—officers, officials, and *colons*—and, at the same time, many interned Moslems whom I knew personally or whose families I knew and who for that reason spoke to me as one speaks to someone who clearly has no hostile prejudices. I can say that the total effect of these conversations presented a coherent image of the situation, whose most striking aspect (I had left Algeria in April 1956) was the importance that the clandestine politi-

---

[4] Published in the United States as *Algeria: The Realities* (New York: Alfred A. Knopf, Inc., 1959).

cal structures had assumed within a year. But even more than this importance, which seemed quite remarkable to me, was what one might call the "style" of the operation (whose lightninglike rapidity of execution was only one of its aspects). I had always thought that a military victory was technically possible in Algeria (one can always neutralize a resistance by annihilating all its organizations, and this can be done regardless of where and in what circumstances, on condition one can pay the price). But it now seemed obvious to me that all the structures would be reconstituted as soon as the military force was reduced.

During the last week of this trip I learned from a Moslem friend that "some people" wanted to ask me questions concerning the brochure I have already mentioned. My friend did not know herself who these people were, but she believed they were important.

In writing this brochure, I had hoped to attract the attention of Moslem public opinion to the extreme danger to Algeria which an unconditional and unlimited independence would present. Moreover, I could easily discuss these conversations with the highest government authority, for M. André Boulloche (at the time director of M. Bourgès-Maunoury's cabinet) had belonged to my Resistance group in 1941; he had been deported along with his father, his brother, and his mother, all of whom died in captivity. M. Louis Mangin, also a member of M. Bourgès-Maunoury's cabinet, and his entire family are among my oldest and closest friends. Further, I was convinced of the futile character of the present struggle as it was being waged on both sides. For all these reasons, I took the responsibility of attending this interview, without knowing whom I was going to meet.

It was arranged that I would follow an Algerian who was indicated to me. He led me by a roundabout route to the place where the meeing was to be held. In fairness to the people who had granted me their confidence, I was careful not to notice the details of the route we had taken.

In the room into which I was shown, I was received by two young women, one of whom (I discovered the day of her arrest) was named Zohra Drif. A few minutes later two men also came in. They were wearing khaki clothes and each was carrying an automatic rifle; I think I remember that they also had one or two revolvers in their belts. The five persons present had not seen one another for many months, it seemed, and greeted one another with emotion. The shorter of the two men was then introduced to me as "Big Brother," then the other man as "our glorious Ali la Pointe." I spoke to the two latest arrivals and we all sat down. There was a brief silence, which I deliberately refrained from breaking; then I said amiably to my interlocutors: "I hear you wanted to see me. Here I am; what do you have to tell me?"

They were obviously surprised, and all eyes turned toward the man they called "Big Brother," who, I learned later, was actually Saadi Yacef. He seemed embarrassed and told me, fumbling somewhat, that having read my brochure, he wanted to ask me several questions about it, but that it would be better for me to talk about such matters with the five members of the C.C.E. (Comité de Coordination et d'Exécution), for they alone were qualified to make any important decision. At the time I knew nothing of the C.C.E.; it was described to me as the organization that directs the clandestine political and military structure of Moslem Algeria. I answered that I could not speak with the members of this organization without my own government's authorization, and I specified on this occasion: "You know that I am neither a communist nor a progressivist,[5] but a patriotic Frenchwoman."

---

[5] After the publication of this testimony, I received several letters from "progressivists" protesting against the opposition I seemed to set up between "patriotism" and "progressivism." It is not my intention to offend anyone, but in my text (intended for the courts of law) I wanted to reproduce *word for word* the conversation which took place on that day. I had delivered this sentence during the first ten minutes of the interview. For I had more or less expected to encounter one or more students armed with spectacles and pens, and I had, in fact, been surprised by the warlike manner and equipment of my interlocutors; that is why I thought I had to specify my own position from the start and without any ambiguity.

The meeting occurred on July 4, 1957, two weeks before the trial of Frenchmen who were accused of having helped the

They all told me in chorus that they were well aware of this and that this was the reason they were so glad to talk to me.

The conversation, which had begun at 2:45 P.M., lasted until 7:30 P.M., and I am going to have to review it as clearly as possible, trying not to distort the sequence. The sequence, as a matter of fact, seems to me of great importance, for it helps show the extremely improvisational character of what was said on either side that day.

Since the interview's point of departure was the brochure I had written about Algeria's social and economic problems, and since no particular question was asked me, I began a long monologue about wages, the necessity of total education, the gradual and inevitable breakdown of the underdeveloped nations, Algeria's inability to subsist without an economic symbiosis with France, and so on. At one point Yacef interrupted me and said thoughtfully: "We aren't accustomed enough to thinking of such things," and on several

---

F.L.N. and whom, for this reason, all the Algerian papers called "progressivists." I did not yet know that the majority of the Frenchmen in question had indeed helped Algerians, but not against France, and were not "progressivists."

With no malevolent intention, I had used the first word that occurred to me in its accepted meaning in Algiers, in order to keep my interlocutors from asking me for help contrary to the interests of my country.

questions he made practical objections that led me
to specify my own position. A little later, in a rather
anxious tone of voice, he asked me: "How do you
think this is all going to end?"

I was quite pessimistic, and I answered grimly:
"There is no reason for it to end. The F.L.N. will
never defeat the French troops, and though the French
troops may stamp out the rebellion temporarily, it
seems impossible to me that they can do so definitively.
If, in some remote future, France grows tired of the
loss of men and money this chronic war represents,
and if she were then to abandon it, it seems to me impossible that the Algerian workers would retain their
present privileges in the French labor market. In that
case, the whole country is doomed to a swift and necessarily bloody regression." I also explained that
though on paper there were eight million Moslems and
slightly over one million Europeans in Algeria—a balance of forces of eight to one—in reality the potential
of any population was not only a question of numbers
but, much more, a result of its technological status and
its investments. In this frame of reference, there was
a kind of balance of forces between the two groups
that made the situation still more of a deadlock: had
there been a lot fewer Europeans, a Tunisian type of
solution would have been possible; had there been a
lot fewer Moslems, the integration programs would
have been achieved without great difficulty; and so on.

It was at this moment that Yacef exclaimed: "Then I'll never be a free man!" His tone was neither hostile nor angry, but genuinely hopeless.

Apropos of the underdeveloped nations, I was led to mention famine, saying that I was the only person in that room who knew exactly how one went about dying of hunger. Then I told a number of personal anecdotes and mentioned the statistics I had accumulated before 1942 on the causes of arrests, describing the informers who had decimated our ranks. "That's the hardest thing to forgive," I said. Yacef interrupted me excitedly. "Oh, if it would only stop, I'd forgive everyone." The conversation then turned for some time to the French Resistance and the sufferings its partisans had endured.

It was then that they began to tell me about the tortures that were inflicted in Algeria and particularly in Algiers. I could answer that I was almost as well informed on this subject as they were, and that this was, in fact, the reason for my present trip. I explained what the International Commission on Internment was. I told them that the non-communist French deportees had requested this investigation, that these deportees belonged to extremely various groups and parties, but that they were all patriots and had not taken this decision lightly; in other words, that their ambition was not to fill the papers with the faults committed by their country, but to bring them to a halt.

I don't know who mentioned Mélouza at one point, but it occasioned one of the rare remarks from the man introduced to me as Ali la Pointe. Speaking vehemently, he said: "It wasn't us!" I answered that he was wrong, for I had just returned from Mélouza and had questioned the survivors myself; I could therefore personally testify that in this case the Fronts' responsibility could not be doubted. His chief then gave him a sign to be still, but I think, nevertheless, it was at this point that I began to discuss the mutilations and murders, about which I was also closely informed. Yacef listened to me with a dismayed expression, but without protesting. I could not help pointing out to him how unfair it was to attribute to a whole group the crimes committed by some of its members, and that what was unfair to him was unfair to us as well. I must say here that during my second trip I learned from one of Yacef's collaborators that Yacef had given orders to stop the barbarous practices of which I have just spoken. I do not know whether these orders were actually given and at what date, but it should be possible to find out.

This portion of the interview lasted more than two hours, and it is likely that had I left at five o'clock as I had planned to, the other questions that were discussed would never have even been mentioned.

My interlocutors listened to me with eager attention and spoke, as I did, with perfect frankness. Moreover, they knew me by reputation and knew that my respect and friendship for their compatriots was longstanding and sincere. Furthermore, my experience of clandestine activities, of our ordeals during the Resistance, fascinated them by the comparisons they made with their own situation. They were also quite aware of the extreme compassion these analogies provoked in me.

Consequently, after about two and a half hours of conversation, Yacef smiled faintly and said something like: "You see that we are neither criminals nor murderers." Very sadly, but very firmly, I answered: "You are murderers." He was so startled that he said nothing for a moment and seemed to be choking. Then his eyes filled with tears and he said: "Yes, Madame Tillion, we are murderers." Then he told me several details about the Casino bombing, adding that when he heard about it he wept for three days and three nights. In this second part of the conversation, he had tears in his eyes on several occasions, and when he spoke of the Casino incident the tears ran down his face.

I remember saying in almost these words: "Terrorism is the justification of the tortures in some people's eyes. To others, the tortures and executions are the justification of terrorism. It is a vicious circle." Another time, Yacef made a sudden gesture and said: "Oh, those bombs, I wish they were all at the bottom of the sea!" I answered that I would be glad to help him throw them there. In a terribly crushed tone he replied: "It's our only way of expressing ourselves." It seems to me that he repeated this phrase several times, and I for my part during this second phase of our conversation repeated: "Innocent blood cries out for vengeance."

From that day on, it was my profound conviction that this man had no intention, in initiating this conversation, of speaking to me of his moral crisis; he had concealed his name from me, as I discovered later, only because it had become a synonym for terrorism in the Algerian papers and because he was afraid of shocking me by telling me who he was. Nevertheless, everything we said was so impromptu that, violating his customary secrecy, he immediately told me the name of his bodyguard (Ali la Pointe), whose reputation was no better than his own.

He expressed himself throughout with a great deal of spontaneity and naturalness, and during our two conversations, thanks to the brief remarks he made, I gained a sense of the kind of life he had been leading for two years, hunted day and night by several thousand soldiers in an area the size of the Jardin du

Luxembourg, making a tremendous physical and intellectual effort almost without material means, for it was his task to co-ordinate first the entire political and military machinery of Algiers and then (as an interim functionary) to ensure this co-ordination for all of Algeria. I could also see the great respect he inspired in his collaborators; yet, precisely because of this respect, they expected him to assume every responsibility in every domain. Consequently, he was obliged to bear a moral burden that had probably been weighing upon him for some time when I met him. The turn our conversation took—quite unexpected to both of us—precipitated, in my opinion, a decision he had already been contemplating a long time.

Almost abruptly he said: "I promise you that from now on we will not touch the civilian population."

I was petrified by this remark, and I answered that I represented no one and that I had no qualifications to accept any such commitment. He answered: "That doesn't matter. It is to you I wish to make this promise, and it is to you that I do make it."

As I said, I am condensing this whole conversation, since it lasted four and a half hours. On several occasions the same subjects were discussed again, and particularly the important one of the connection between the terrorist attacks on the one hand and the French executions on the other.

Quite a long time after the unilateral promise that had been made to me, I said, apropos of these executions: "But if there are more executions, will you still keep your promise?" Saadi Yacef then made a violent gesture and said: "In that case, I cannot answer for anything."

I had already realized that in cases of capital punishment the pressure of Moslem public opinion is so strong on the clandestine organizations that they are *obliged* (in order to manifest their presence and their community of feeling with the mass of the people) to take action.

Incidentally, during the conversation I said that I considered myself obliged to report this discussion to my government. Yacef shrugged and said: "Do whatever you want. It doesn't matter to us," and he added that, as far as he was concerned, all he wanted was that I should be able to discuss Algeria's economic problems with the five C.C.E. leaders. In his mind, the essential purpose of that discussion was the instruction of the men responsible, in his opinion, for the direction Algeria would take with regard to problems that to him seemed very serious and inadequately considered by Moslem public opinion in general. But he stressed several times the fact that his opinion in the matter didn't count. I could agree to provide explanations in these areas only on condition that my government authorized me to do so.

. . .

Around seven-thirty I ended the interview. At the moment of leaving I turned first toward the two young women sitting on my right. The young blonde (Zohra Drif) had spoken briefly on one or two occasions; the other woman had taken no part in the conversation. Consequently, I did not know how they felt about this long discussion. I shook hands with them, and when one of them kissed me, I realized their emotion and, deeply touched myself, said: "I beg you to use your influence to protect the innocent." Both bowed their heads gravely. I then turned toward the man called Ali la Pointe and, seizing him by his shirt collar, I shook him a little and said: "Did you understand what I said? Innocent blood cries out for vengeance!" Somewhat intimidated, he answered: "Yes, m'dame." Lastly I shook hands with Saadi Yacef. He took my hand in both of his and said with emotion: "Thank you for having spoken to us as you have." Then I left with the guide, and, as I did the first time, I took care not to notice the route we followed.

This interview had taken place on July 4. The following Saturday, the sixth, I flew to Paris with the other members of the Commission, and on Monday, July 8, I gave a faithful account of the conversation to my friends on the President's Council. I ended with my personal view of the Algerian problem: that the hysteria of both populations constitutes an almost absolute obstacle to any solution; that it will be necessary to devise some means of regulating the conflict (acceptable to both groups), but—whatever this means is—that it can be applied only after the level of mutual hatred and terror is reduced. The European population is justifiably terrified by the attacks; they provoke the most violent reactions among the Europeans, which are precisely contrary to the goal desired: to make the attacks stop. It is consequently under the pressure of fear and horror that the European population demands (through its avowed or secret representatives) executions, arrests, innumerable cruelties. These have as their goal the annihilation of the adversary, but so long as they do not achieve this goal, they have, apparently, a direct influence on the increase in the number of attacks; and if they ultimately manage to achieve their goal, it can only be temporarily. Conversely, the Moslem population, which, almost unanimously, considers those men condemned to death national heroes, is roused to a state of violent aggression and despair each time the death sentence is carried out. The people then demand the terrorist reaction, though it provokes a repression of which the Moslem population is necessarily the first victim. If the Algerian nationalists had totally abstained from attacks upon the civilian population, there might have been only a few cases of torture. Inversely, if the French

Army, perfectly under control, had been able to refrain from any excesses, there might have been only a few attacks. Yet it is because each side has indulged in an unlimited rivalry that the situation has been continually aggravated. Starting from this point of view, I suggested suspending the executions for as long as there were no attacks, and I was informed that my suggestion would be considered, for it seemed, at first sight, quite reasonable.

In a second conversation, the President of the Council's cabinet director told me that the government had wanted for a long time to know the true viewpoint of the Front's politico-military leaders, and that it also hoped to discuss with them the prospects France envisaged for Algeria. It was not a question of negotiation, but of a private conversation, which could, eventually—if the viewpoints were not too discordant—give rise to precise deliberation. With this in view, I would have to agree to return to Algeria to speak to a member of the C.C.E.; and I would also have to agree to do this at my own risk.

I was well aware of what this risk meant, but I agreed nevertheless, partly out of patriotism and partly because of the extreme compassion I felt for the miseries of the Algerian people. I attached only one condition to my acceptance, which was that I would in no way be used without my knowledge to deceive the people I would meet, who would be trusting me. The President of the Council's cabinet director gave me his word of honor on this matter and I had no further objection, for I had complete confidence in his good faith. However, I took every possible precaution to keep our meeting from endangering any of my interlocutors, for that was the *sine qua non* of my acceptance.

I set the date of departure of my second trip for Wednesday, July 24, because on that day the monitors of the Social Centers, which had been created under my responsibility, were to be tried in Algiers. I wanted to be there in case, though acquitted and freed, they nevertheless found themselves in danger, as has occasionally happened in Algiers during these last months.

The Saturday before I left I had an interview with one of my friends, M. Louis Mangin, who informed me, with great circumspection, that three executions were going to take place in Algiers at once.

This news came as a great shock to me, not only because it meant the immediate resumption of attacks against an innocent population and, in the long run, a widening of the trench of hatred separating the two communities a little more each day, but also because I am particularly sensitive in this area.

Two of my Resistance comrades were arrested in

February 1941; from February 1941 to February 1942
I tried to organize their defense and obtain their pardon; on the eve of their execution, one of the lawyers
asked me to inform the families, and at the end of the
terrible day itself, still unwilling to believe in the
worst, I attempted to take further steps to save them,
although they had already been shot. And on the next
day another lawyer gave me the journal of one of the
dead men, which revealed in detail the treachery that
had betrayed them all to the Gestapo. The steps I
took to eliminate the traitor and organize the escape
of three other men condemned to death were the
cause of my own arrest, which occurred on Friday,
August 13, 1942. For several months, and several times
a week, I then had occasion to say farewell to comrades
who were taken to the execution stake, and the indignation, the fury, and the grief I felt then are still
alive in me today.

Thus, in the presence of a population which I know
particularly well, where I have countless friends and
have always been received with complete trust, and
whose ordeals, moreover, have always been familiar
to me (they did not start yesterday), it was impossible
for me not to recognize feelings that I myself have
felt. I shared their suffering doubly.

Nevertheless, I had agreed to go, and I flew to Algiers three days later. Yet I left terrified by the inco-

herence of our policy, with no hopes for a possibility of reconciliation, and sick at heart.

The very evening of my arrival—that is, on July 24 —I learned the verdict rendered in the trial which had ended on that day. I even had the opportunity to meet one of the lawyers who had pleaded and several of the persons acquitted or released in the case. Despite all I already knew of it, I was stunned by the facts which, quite discreetly but officially, this trial had revealed (disappearances and tortures, which the victims' innocence—admitted by the tribunal—rendered still more intolerable).

The next day, while meeting with a group of lawyers, I learned that during the night the three executions which I had been told about had taken place; one of the lawyers had been present.

The day after, a Saturday, eight bombs exploded in Algiers. When they exploded, I happened to be not far away from one of them, and I immediately hastened to the scene of the attack to find out if it had been made against civilians, for I had decided, if this was the case, to return to Paris at once. I am neither a diplomat nor a soldier, and no one could force me to continue this mission against my will. I was determined not to pursue it if I could not obtain an immediate cessation of the attack-tortures-executions cycle. This was, on my part, an act of obviously in-

stinctive repulsion, but it was also justified on the
level of reason, for no chance of concluding anything
in human terms remained if there was no trace of an
active desire for peace, or even simply of a little good
faith and humanity on either side.

I learned the next day that there had been no civilian victims (which I attributed, at the time, to an
extraordinary piece of luck), and I therefore agreed to
the meeting which had been planned between a representative of the C.C.E. and myself. (This meeting, if
it had taken place, would have had the character of a
free discussion on both sides of social and economic
problems.) But, contrary to the arrangements made
early in July, no member of the C.C.E. could be
reached at the beginning of August, for because of the
imminence of the United Nations debates, all members would be outside Algeria at this time. It was
therefore decided that before leaving I would have a
second conversation with Saadi Yacef. It was then
that I learned his name.

This second conversation took place on Friday, August 9. I had made it clear in advance that I would be
speaking only for myself, but with the authorization
of my government. No less clearly, Saadi Yacef had
informed me that any decision relating to a possibility
of negotiation was the exclusive responsibility of the

C.C.E. Our second meeting, then, had as its particular purpose to prepare for a third—if the members of
the C.C.E. were willing to follow up the suggestion
that Yacef had taken the responsibility of making to
them.

He arrived, as he did the first time, with his automatic rifle in his hand but quite relaxed and smiling.
He began by saying: "I heard you escaped an attack."
Very coldly I answered: "If there had been a single
civilian victim, I should not be here, for I would have
packed my bag at once and returned to Paris. We can
thank God." In the same free and easy tone he answered: "I knew that, and as a result I had taken
every precaution. It is not God you should thank, but
me." I then said to him very seriously: "You are right,
monsieur, and I do thank you. I thank you all the
more because I know that on our side nothing has
been done in the human direction I desired."

As at the first conversation, Zohra Drif was present,
but she took a larger part in it this time, and since we
were all speaking only for ourselves, we approached
every problem with perfect frankness and great freedom of expression. We spoke first of the various prospects for a possible agreement and of the likelihood of
discussing them with the members of the C.C.E. On
this occasion Yacef said: "If I receive the order to do
so, it will take me forty-eight hours to call a cease-fire

over the entire extent of Algeria." Then he reflected
a moment and added: "It will take me three days."
Regarding the decision itself, it rested, in his opinion
—and he held to it in advance—exclusively with the
only organization whose authority he recognized, the
C.C.E. His own role was to insure throughout Algeria
the co-ordination of military and political action—a
role for which, however, as I understood it, he had
no accounting to make to anyone. As for his personal
opinions (which he always expressed with a great deal
of spontaneity), they seemed to me full of good sense
and moderate, while remaining loyal to a firm ideal.

Familiar with Algerian society and the surprising
contradictions within the present situation, I was not
shocked to hear him express several times a real at-
tachment to France and to French civilization and
culture: I heard him speak fondly of Paris and sym-
pathetically about our young people. During these
two very long conversations when I insisted on the
necessity of an economic symbiosis between the two
nations, he expressed the ardent desire that once the
goal of freedom was achieved, close links could at last
be established and consolidated between our two peoples, and he did not conceal from me the suspicion he
felt toward the governments and organizations which
could derive a profit from their chronic misunderstanding. It was clear that he assessed the difficulties

of complete independence realistically, though independence constituted an ideal for which (he also told me several times) he had agreed to die.

The next day (Saturday, August 10), I went to reserve a seat on the first plane back to Paris. Since it was the vacation season, I could obtain one only for two days later, and on Sunday I heard from Moslems that there had been two new executions in Algiers.

They did not conceal their fear and their horror at the thought of the reprisals that these executions could not fail to provoke. I knew the situation well enough at the time to be convinced that it was no longer possible to avoid them. Nevertheless, I decided to write a letter to Saadi Yacef, begging him to take the responsibility of stopping this murderous rivalry, but—since it had been impossible for me to halt this savage and stupid machinery on the French side—I asked him to be generous and intelligent enough to take this position of moderation *alone and unilaterally*.

After receiving this letter he informed me that there would be no reprisals, and there were none.

Now, I wish to state that on this date, August 11, 1957, all F.L.N. organizations knocked out in February–April had been reconstituted and that in their new form they were still intact (as was indicated by the arrests that were made several weeks later and by

the documents discovered at that time and published
by the press).

As a consequence, my personal conviction is that
not only did Saadi Yacef intend to stop the attacks
against the French civilian population, but he *actually
did stop them*, and he did so throughout Algeria. My
conviction is based on the immediate, general, and apparently inexplicable cessation of terrorism on the date
of July 4,[6] which is that of the first interview I had with
Yacef, and the attempted resumption of terrorism immediately after his arrest, which took place on Tuesday, September 25.[7]

---

[6] June 5, 1957. *Le Monde* (after the June 3 attacks): "Information from Algiers indicates an increasing anxiety in the
civilian population. It is being asked if the results obtained
this winter by General Massu are not negated."

July 4, 1957. Yacef's promise to spare the civilian population.

July 12, 1957. *Paris-Presse*. Headline: WHAT DOES THIS
SUDDEN TRUCE CONCEAL? "(*From our special correspondent
Jean Taousson*.) *Algiers, July 11*. The sudden truce that has
marked these last few days seems extraordinary to the Frenchmen of Algeria. It is a fact that for over a week the rebels have
shown their hand only occasionally."

July 12, 1957. *L'Echo d'Alger*. Headline on page 1: M.
LACOSTE IN THE MINISTERIAL COUNCIL: DISTINCT REGRES-
SION OF TERRORISM.

July 17, 1957. *L'Echo d'Alger*. Headline on page 1: THE
F.L.N. HAS EXECUTED LOUNIS MEKHLAF, THE GUNMAN
WHO PLANTED HIS BOMB IN THE CASINO DE LA CORNICHE.

[7] October 1, 1957. *Le Monde*. Headline: BRUTAL REVIVAL

I am also convinced that Yacef desired and achieved this sudden and general halt for specifically moral reasons—in order to spare the innocent—and I base this conviction on the evidence of his extreme emotion when he revealed (in a completely spontaneous way, I believe) his painful moral debate. However, his purely political opinions (on the interdependence linking the French and Algerian populations, on their need to treat each other with circumspection and to find grounds for mutual understanding) and his profound and sincere desire that negotiations achieve results, certainly helped reinforce his decision and eventually justify it among his colleagues and within the F.L.N., whose power he recognized in making any decision (in other words, the C.C.E.).

A close reading of the Algerian press during July, August, September, and October 1956 has only confirmed my profound certainty, revealing previous projects[8] that were radically and abruptly modified after the meeting I have just reported, without any new fact in the interval being able to explain this reversal.

OF TERRORISM. "*Algiers, September 30*. After several weeks of relative calm, a brutal outbreak of terrorism has occurred in several villages in the departments of Constantine and Oran."
[8] August 30, 1957. *L'Echo d'Alger*. Headline on page 1: Two HELD: COLLABORATORS OF SAADI YACEF ARRESTED. On the same day, documents seized on August 27 were published; they called for "bomb attacks" from August 24 to August 31, and from August 1 to August 8 for "more attacks in sites more carefully chosen."

.   .   .

Saadi Yacef was condemned to death three times by the military tribunal of Algiers in 1958: on June 25, on July 4, and on August 25. The second trial was appealed, and was confirmed on October 27 of the same year.

Saadi Yacef was saved by the general amnesty that General de Gaulle, upon his election to the presidency of the Republic, granted to all those condemned to death.

PART 2

1960

The War for Nothing

A revolution organized into a permanent institution, a permanent army of half a million men, two counterrevolutions in twenty months—this makes a lot of diseases for a nation of ten million inhabitants already devastated by cruel poverty.

A great modern and prosperous nation, the first to proclaim the equality of men and make itself the champion of their freedom, has over a period of fifteen years fought ruinous wars contrary to her own nature, her internal equilibrium, her international interests, against peoples asking her for their independence. She thereby risks losing her own twice over.

The causes of such pernicious damage deserve to be analyzed, for they are not comprehensible if we do not examine piece by piece the mechanisms of our country and the strange and ambivalent relations it maintains with the two populations disputing the direction Algeria will take.

This effort is necessary, for all these cruel evils have only one cure: it is called reconciliation.

Yet a reconciliation cannot exist without justice—a justice of nations and a justice of men, the one guaranteeing the other, both equally indispensable for containing the flood of horrors that the madness of politics and the madness of war have loosed.

I

The "Frenchmen of the Interior" [1]

> Now, as for these people whose destiny
> was restored and who were not, I think,
> incapable of freely choosing the right
> path, what have we done to furnish
> them the minimum of sure and clear
> information without which any rational
> conduct is impossible?
>
> —Marc Bloch:
> *L'Etrange Défaite*, July 1940

THE FRANCE of 1960 is rich; Frenchmen work hard
and work well; they have fertile fields, new machines,
many healthy children, an international audience—but
apparently they don't know how to govern themselves.

Yet we are neither more stupid nor more wicked
than the inhabitants of other nations, who manage to
permit the coexistence of a state and public liberties.
The overwhelming majority of us desire order and
peace, and we wish to live as a democracy—yet we

---

[1] The Frenchmen of Alsace have preserved the custom of
calling by this name the Frenchmen living west of the Vosges.
This chapter includes portions of an article called "La France
en miettes," which appeared in *Preuves* (June and July 1960)
and whose title had been adopted by analogy with that of
Georges Friedman's study *Le Travail en miettes* (Paris: Gal-
limard, 1956).

wage war, to the great danger of our order and our democracy.

Some attribute our difficulties to particular national and even hereditary defects, and trace them back to the chaos of which our ancestors the Gauls are said to furnish the original example. Contrary to the theory, it seems to me that the extreme complication of our political life derives more from phenomena of "modernism" than from ancient national disputes. On these grounds that complication threatens all nations on our level.

We, and the Others

In any archaic society (Provençal village or African tribe, it doesn't matter) one is struck by the multiplicity and vitality of the relations that bind the members of the group together. Solidarity, generosity—but also unlimited indiscretion, constant pressure on the individual's desires, tastes, and aspirations. Modern man is, in part, freed from this pressure, but at the same time deprived—and harshly—of the reassuring warmth of the herd. Freed: like a boat without a pilot. At the mercy of the current.

I have known societies in Europe, in Africa, in America, where people of all ages still divided their leisure hours between tall stories and inexhaustible family gossip. There is every reason to suppose that the nine hundred generations separating us from the paleolithic era had few other subjects to enliven their evenings— first in caves, later in huts, even palaces.

In our time, in the chic apartments of the XVI arrondissement as in the housing projects of the suburbs, great numbers of city dwellers have been prematurely cut off from the fascinating gossip of the ancestral clan and from its fairy tales. Imprisoned in an emotional poverty which is the seamy side of the modern world, they are left with the agony columns—a combination of gossip and the supernatural—to beguile their failure, their solitude. (I am not speaking of the multitudes gathered in the African shanty towns—they are still assiduously plagued by spirits and mothers-in-law—but of our own people who, at a higher level of development, must nourish themselves exclusively on royal births and California divorces.)

The modern nation tends, as a matter of fact, toward increasing centralization (a tendency reinforced by all the present mechanisms of transportation and information). This centralization accelerates with agricultural modernization, industrialization, urbanization, commercialization, while the populations increase more rapidly and shift en masse.

All these phenomena, multiplied together, break off the traditional relations between individuals. Other relations are created—for man cannot live without them—but these are still sketchy, and consequently unstable and rather incoherent. Besides, they do not eliminate the old ones, but are superimposed upon them, and not without occasional contradictions. I refer to the relations which are formed within each nation, but which also transcend these nations, penetrate them, and bind them to one another.

Each human being's conception of the relations—both real and ideal—that unite or oppose him to the rest of humanity is the profound basis of his personality.

Once—and that situation still survives, here and there—humanity was divided into two coherent and stable groups: *We* and *the Others*.

We: an entity not to be judged, or seen, and in which each individual melts like a piece of sugar in hot coffee; *the Others*: unknown monsters who don't talk "like everyone else," who eat disgusting food, who pray the wrong way, who dress absurdly, do unexpected things . . .

I have known French villages where *the Others* was the next village and also the rest of the world. I have known Algerian tribes who, in the same way, quite simply divided the whole universe in two; in the *mechta* on the mountaintop, an insuperable barrier of fear threatened any individual not linked by a formal alliance, but—more than all the rest—it haloed with disturbing gleams the inhabitants of the village below.

The world over, this is gradually becoming a thing of the past.

In 1960, what is *We?* We French? We workers? We intellectuals? We owners of fifty acres? We officials of such and such a grade? We African Negroes, or Senegalese, or citizens of Mali? We champions of the West against the other cardinal points of the compass? We Marxists? We pacifists? We career soldiers? We Mormons?

Of course, danger unifies, simplifies; from 1939 to 1945 we could say "We Frenchmen," just as in the last six years every man in Algeria, one by one, has learned to say "We Algerians." But misfortunes and dangers pass (fortunately!), and we must still learn how to live in the (complicated) circumstances of security and comfort.

When hierarchies and structures, administrations, political parties, and even the simplest choices, the indispensable ligaments, are fragmented, disjointed, like a cargo badly stowed on a pitching boat, the public weighs down the side already sinking, and can accelerate a shipwreck.

We humans

Humanity has increasing difficulty co-ordinating an ancestral equilibrium, obviously empirical, with a sud-

denly excessive power and growing human masses that
are badly or not at all adjusted to one another. Inter-
dependences multiply, and attain an extent and a complexity that the people they link cannot even succeed
in conceiving.

In all material things, instruments henceforth sub-
stitute for us, but for human affairs instruments become as deceptive as those who employ them. In other
words, all we have is still only our judgment—the trust
we accord here, refuse there.

Some are surprised to see, in every nation of the
earth—Marxist and democratic, archaic and modern,
old monarchies and new republics—the crowds shame-
lessly abandoning themselves to their local "cult of
personality."

It is easy to criticize, but *when millions of individuals are doing the same thing at the same time, it
seems more useful, and more rational, to wonder why
they are doing it,* particularly since, by a contradiction
that is only apparent, when each individual finds himself defenseless before the catastrophes of our time, the
weight of public opinion is becoming overwhelming.

Between their fearful weight and the fragile and
permeable element that constitutes them (that is, modern man, in his abandonment, his vulnerability, his solitude), the instruments of transmission and co-ordination reveal their inadequacy: the gigantic states of the

twentieth century constantly increase their power and hurl themselves with mounting speed down slopes that grow ever steeper—but they have preserved, without improving them, the couplings of the last century. They have not even preserved them, for rust is corroding them.

A powerful and free press would certainly help matters.

To seek out the truth—where, when, and how a thing happened, and to tell it without distortion—assumes a world-wide importance that increases in proportion to the falsifying ingenuity of various propaganda. Yet this requires the experience and the authority possessed by a very small number of great journalists.

The weight of the press, the authority of the men who have our confidence, can grow only at the same rate as the increase in the number of the earth's inhabitants: not like a weed in fallow land, the stubborn squitch grass that takes advantage of the cultivator's negligence to choke the wheat, but like the grain that ultimately fills the fields because it corresponds to an elementary and vital need which it alone can sustain.

By intuition or empiricism, the American democracy does not begrudge the press this vital place which is its due. In France—a modern nation resting on an ancient and hard pedestal—the strain between the day before yesterday and the day after tomorrow is more violent than elsewhere; our press is often its victim, and our governments have too easy a tendency to bully it, to lack respect for it, while even public opinion does not gauge the importance of its role.

The press and its eminent rights should everywhere be consolidated, reinforced, for it is the transmission belt which supplies all these fine networks binding men to stable and vital communities.

Today belt and network are unraveling under the clumsy feet of the enormous girl who has too quickly gobbled down the mushroom that makes her grow. Like Alice in Wonderland, humanity, suddenly stricken with gigantism, has retained its baby's brain; but, less fortunate than Alice, its little panties and its apron have not grown along with it, and it finds itself —half naked, terrified, enormous—clutching its bread and butter, which has also grown no larger.

The once hermetic partitions that separated nations are everywhere collapsing, and there no longer exists any national problem, insignificant or serious, which fails to echo beyond the borders of the nation directly involved.

This bumper cotton or coffee crop, that surplus of petroleum or olive oil, are felt around the world. When an influenza epidemic strikes in Italy, people soon begin coughing in Lyon, in Paris, and in London; when cases of smallpox are announced in Moscow, it is wise to be vaccinated in Rome, in New York, and in Peking. Similarly, when a shot is fired in Formosa, in the Middle East, in the Forum of Algiers, the reverberations move outward, ring by ring.

National dramas are propagated in waves, overrunning the dikes and, like waves, returning in the opposite direction—thereby aggravating their eddies.

Innumerable misfortunes, as frightening as earthquakes or epidemics, but of human origin, have made their appearance and now more than ever threaten every single man.

Every human being hopes with all his heart to avoid atomic conflict, but what is the best way to avoid this disaster? Mr. Dulles's "calculated risk"? The stormy encounters of the present cycle?

The peoples of the world, scarred by a series of historical calamities, obviously prefer the "warm peace" to the old "cold war"—but the same honest Americans who followed Mr. Dulles have subsequently followed the opposite policy, and in Russia, Stalin probably enjoyed approval quite as sincere as that showered on Mr. Khrushchev today. On all sides people advance timidly toward the tempting shores of peace—anxiously inspecting every bush, every shadow, ready at the first alarm to fling themselves back into the water.

Above this figured bass, minor themes run through

the earthly harmony: Berlin (or Palestine, or Formosa, or the Sikkim, or somewhere), "zone of free exchange," "common market," O.E.E.C. . . .

In these various domains, technicians have contradictory opinions; you can sort them out only if you're something of a technician yourself. It is really too much to ask of people who work more than eight hours a day, often far from their homes, wracked by problems of health or family—in short: our modern electors.

Among them, how many know, even vaguely, what such words stand for? No doubt very few. All, on the other hand, are aware of the presence, beyond their horizons, of enormous mysterious clouds, heavy with a horrible, particularly destructive dust. But what winds push them, or push them back, and what influences will they exert over such obsessive and familiar problems as the cost of living, unemployment, recession?

The number of potential catastrophic combinations at the national and international levels continues to increase. Anyone can interrupt (or seriously perturb) the course of anyone else's life. We must make swifter decisions, or suffer still more dramatic consequences whose sum constitutes a multifarious, obsessive, permanent danger which concerns us all and against which each of us feels even more helpless than against the damages of brute nature.

And nevertheless—on the positive side of the ledger

—this intrusion of the great world within every fron-tier is giving birth, amid its increasing confusion, to a sense—still faint, still obscure—of a solidarity among the earth's inhabitants.

Transcending nations and policies, many men of every walk of life, of every nationality, of every faith, already say or think "We humans" and are moved by the sufferings of a bleeding flesh that each of them would once have called "foreign." Henceforth, the more a nation appears to be torn by irreconcilable choices, by rending tensions, the wider it will open, in many hearts, to this transcending of nations, the condition of the survival of our race.

Volume Two of human history

While the huge modern nations, confused and un-wieldy, evolve with difficulty their increasingly supra-national policies, no leader of a major state can him-self give all the orders that his function and his plans require; none can even keep informed of everything he needs to know. Threatened with total paralysis, these gigantic organisms must therefore possess a general line of conduct clear and simple enough to be well defined, inculcated, and understood at every level.

The old "reasons of state" are still there, but they have proliferated in proportion to the general com-

plexity of modern societies; they have therefore become numberless and contradictory—"lunacies of
state" that are taken less and less seriously, despite
their noisiness. Besides, as audiences have widened,
lies are increasingly exposed to the possibility of not
being believed.

Pinned together by agreements that multiply and
plague them from without, constituted of tiny hard,
smooth kernels that a crumbling mortar has difficulty
holding together, the democratic states are fragile, and
they find their strength only in their program. Yet this
program could be a factor of equilibrium, for if it were
scrupulously pursued, it would find accomplices in
each of the earth's three billion inhabitants—three
billion tiny invisible "stabilizers" known as love of life,
of happiness, of peace . . .

If the democracies want to survive, they must pay a
great deal of attention to their weaknesses (inherent
in their nature, and undeniable), but also to their
strengths, which they waste by trying to imitate the
"effective" states.

Their opportunity is to be in fact what they promise—that is, to be just: to maintain liberty, equality,
brotherhood, as the bases of their laws, and in every
circumstance to make the rights of the human being
respected.

Among the racket of republics being born and dying

and of the wars that succeed one another —insidiously,
one age has reached its term, another is born, and the
age of steel makes way for the nuclear age, while billions of men replace millions—two forces, the atom
and the multitude, have in less than twenty years up-
set our entire historical experience.

Dismayed by brand-new systems of references,
clinging to outdated analogies, France had the misfortune to be questioned without adequate prepara-
tion on a difficult problem of Volume Two of human
history. Unfortunately for her, tomorrow had already
begun.

The French

The divorce between the leaders of public opinion
and that public itself seems wider in France than in
any other nation of the world. In Algeria particularly,
the crowds are good-tempered, insofar as they follow
their leaders without too many zigzags—that is, the
F.L.N. for the Moslems, and the *ultra* organizations
for the populations of so-called French stock.

As for the "Frenchmen of the Interior," they do
not follow, or follow very slowly, and they miss most
of the curves.

Many people who are, as we say, *engagé*, on the
Right as on the Left, complain of this situation and

accuse the body of our compatriots of being indifferent, ignorant, selfish, and so forth. Yet it seems to me we have been offered the spectacle of the extraordinary progress that "public affairs" has made in contaminating the majority of private lives in the last few years.

Then why this inertia?

To answer this question correctly would mean devoting my time to a specific study, and that is not my intention. At best, I can enumerate the circumstances that might have influenced this state of affairs, multiplying contradictory tensions.

Moreover, it is not impossible that these causes of divisions simply furnish a nation the opportunity to become aware of a more essential confusion that relates to our time. In this multiplicity of obligations, both domestic and external, which burden states today, in this technological proliferation which necessarily preoccupies them, the most useful effort for the common good would be for each politician to make his choices comprehensible to his sovereign, the people. In order to control increasing complications, this effort must increase as well. It seems inadequate, at present, as much in France as abroad.

Chosen by electors who are manifestly uncertain, the party that controls Parliament finds itself imprisoned in formulated programs—the capital-labor conflict, secularization, Europe, decolonization, to cite only the most obvious (to which must be added a certain number of personal vendettas).

All of this provokes periodic schisms and a new series of initials increasingly difficult to identify.

Our politics increasingly becomes an affair of initiates, of technicians, of professionals who, without paying any attention to what is happening, let themselves be confined in tiny esoteric circles, some of which reach power—a power, of course, tempered by the chronic non-obedience of the administration. Once the party is in power, it finds itself in conflict both with its own principles and with the people who have elected it. Meanwhile the mass of the country continues to endure—without a means of parrying (though not without irritation)—the innumerable itches of the "nations known as fortunate."

People who consider these phenomena from outside are inclined to criticize the rigor of the principles and the apparent lack of realism which separate the French leaders from the rest of the nation, and they sympathize with our overworked and outdistanced masses.

But this attitude, too, is not necessarily valid; in difficult cases, like that of the reconstruction of Europe, of the construction of the peace, or of decolonization, a small number of men must sail our ship of state against the current of public opinion, for the greatest good of the greatest number. The masses follow, with greater or lesser delays.

Two tendencies (or perhaps two human types) necessarily exist within each party: on one side, there is an effort to mold the masses according to a program; on the other, the program is manipulated to adapt it to the preferences of the majority. In periods of crisis, these two tendencies constitute an additional element of disintegration, which will not spare even so monolithic a party as the Communist party.

There exists no rule for settling this conflict; the masses are violent, ignorant, secretly racist—and yet they are right more often than the "specialists." Perhaps, on the whole, humanity contains a tiny bit more wisdom than foolishness, a tiny bit less nastiness than kindness. This would explain why, in every nation on earth, we have come to the conclusion that many men together make fewer mistakes than only a few men. In any case, innumerable proverbs affirm this wisdom.

If we accept this optimistic hypothesis, we must still not forget that the margin is an extremely narrow one and that statistically we still have many chances for error. Living is not a science, but an art, and a little insight is worth more than any rule.

Our nation, however, for the last fifteen years, has been confronted by a phenomenon of which it cannot remain merely a spectator, for it is caught in the dispute even before it has realized what is involved. I refer to decolonization.

It appeared at first under the aspect of difficulties

that were badly explained, ambiguous, bitter, humiliating.

These causes of dissatisfaction merely added to a long series of divisions and confusions that it is rather tiresome to list. In short, like every democratic nation, during the nineteenth century France had two parties, a monarchist Right, which was afterward called "conservative," and a republican Left, which, after the elimination of our various monarchies, was called "radical," then "socialist." Both still survive, but without being exactly superimposed on our modern partisans of Western and Eastern blocs—which gives us two Lefts: the group of socialist Lefts and the communist Left; and two Rights: an Americanophile Right and an Americanophobe Right.

The terrible ordeal of the German occupation divided the French along lines that did not correspond to the old parties, but the reactionary orientation of the Vichy regime severely compromised the old Right.

Consequently, it was the Left that breasted the waves, and precisely because of an impulse that was favorable to it at the liberation; as a result, it found itself courted on either side: on one by the sudden extension of the Communist party, on the other by a new Catholic Popular party (M.R.P.).

When we analyze the political behavior of electors confronted with complex choices, we realize, in fact, that the "program," the "content," of each party escapes them and that they cling to relative positions: "more" than radical means socialist; "more" than socialist means communist; and so on.

In this perspective, a general impulsion to the Left increases the net weight of the party furthest to the Left (the Communist), thanks to votes withdrawn from the socialist, which swell, in return, the radical seats. The same impulsion increases the consistency, within the old Catholic Right, of a liberal and republican Christian wing. This latter will support the old Left (socialist, radical, anti-clerical) in every area save that of education; consequently, one need only reawaken the question of secularization in order to force the democratic parties to choose between an association with the Communist party or a resignation to the advantage of the extreme Right.

Since May 13, 1958,[2] we have seen a move to the Right analogous in its mechanism to the move to the Left that followed the liberation. Analogous, too, in its results: an increase in the confusion of French politics.

It proceeded from a double ambiguity; it is difficult to see how it could have been avoided.

In 1946, lacking a majority support in the Parliament, General de Gaulle found it impossible to oppose the constitution that was adopted. He took this defeat sufficiently to heart to withdraw from politics—

---

[2] For other aspects of May 13, 1958, see below, Chapter IV.

with reason, for this failure had major consequences. Once he agreed to return to public life, one could be sure he would not let himself be caught in the same trap again.

In 1958, despite an evident reluctance, he therefore let himself be more or less monopolized by one party or other, trying of course to attach it to himself, not himself to it, but naturally without complete success.

We call "great characters" those who don't do what they don't want to do—or at least not often. To do what they want takes, besides luck, patience.

The French, for their part, followed—and still follow—General de Gaulle. Their reasons are varied and many, but they have one in common: *they know him,* and, if my reader has followed me this far, he will realize that this reason itself is a decisive one.

In short, they did what they could, in 1958, to keep him: they voted for the party that seemed most likely to support the policy of a man who inspired confidence. The result has pitched the ship of state far to the Right. The French then discovered themselves rigged out with a whole apparatus which vexed them just as much as the preceding ones—and which dismayed them as well.

For the first time in eighty years, they had elected a resolutely reactionary Parliament (quickly jammed, it was true, between General de Gaulle—a statesman of liberal opinions and authoritarian character—and

electors who, strangely enough, supported the government against their own deputies).

In this freakish situation, the nation's anti-parlia-
mentarian elements (and particularly several military
organizations) found an exceptional support in a Parliament which they dreamed of eliminating, while
they collided head on against the "strong government"
that was their cherished ideal.

The Left, too, found itself caught between the
deputies trying to exterminate it (though the Left
represents their natural support) and what it has particularly feared for a century and a half: the conjunction of a great man and a public opinion that supports
him too unconditionally.

When, in 1958, France had to deal with the *inevitable* ordeal—the revision of values signified by the
word "decolonization"—she numbered 27,350,000 electors, to which should be added two or three million
young men and women not yet voting but much
more articulate than the oldest voters. In 1951, the
total number of electors abstaining represented 19.8
per cent of the electoral body; seven years later, in
1958, abstentions reached 22.9 per cent, and in January 1961, 23.5 per cent.

Among those who vote—that is, 72.5 to 80 per cent
of the registered electors—how many belong to a
party?

It is difficult to know with any precision. Still, we

know that in the organized groups, the number of those registered shrinks each year, and that on the day of the vote, when a party is in fashion, it can count on a hundred times more votes than the number of its contributing members. In bad times, it loses about twenty times more votes than it has members.

According to these data, we may suppose that among the serious electors—those who make the effort of voting—at most two out of a hundred are registered in a party and at least 20 per cent vote for that party with apparent loyalty.

The rest (some 80 per cent of the people who bother to go, on Sunday, to drop a slip in an electoral urn) apparently vote in an impromptu manner. If we add to these the discouraged who don't vote at all, we get a figure close to 85 per cent of the registered elements.

The parties along with the newspapers (those that constitute them and those that read them, and read them attentively), represent an informed but extremely divided public opinion. The number of individuals composing it seems quite low, probably less than 2 per cent of the French public.

In case of a great crisis, this *informed* public opinion, too weak numerically, finds itself overrun. In normal times the influences it exerts and those it endures are more or less balanced.

To ignore "unformed" opinion for the sake of "in-

formed" opinion was the fatal mistake of the Fourth
Republic. The Fifth Republic ignores the informed
minorities as well.

In May 1958, the people who telephoned me from
minute to minute (comrades from the Resistance or
from captivity) were friends of such long standing
that their exact positions, in the confusion of the moment, were familiar to me. They were all extremely
eager to "do something." Yet those who wanted to
rush to the aid of "France in danger" had not stopped
being (I knew) faithful and loyal republicans, and
those who wanted to "save the Republic" remained
patriots. Nevertheless, the logic of the event induced
them to oppose each other to the point of violence.[3]

January 1960 brought a new crisis, in which all the
populations of Algeria panicked. The wing of the cy-
clone crossed the sea and brushed certain of our administrations—the only ones to flinch—while, in a
unanimity as broad as it was brief, the French, astonished and rather pleased to be in agreement, regrouped
around General de Gaulle to defend the unity of their
country. Consequently, there was no need of the
state's usual bridles. This was a very fortunate thing.

The weakening of the parties and the Parliament,
and the strong hostility that exists in France against
them, constitute one of the great dangers of the pres-

---

[3] I urged them to do nothing of the kind.

ent moment, but not the only one, for we observe analogous havoc within all our administrations. Since 1958 there has also been frequent mention of the pressure the Algerian colonels applied to the generals, and of the pressure these colonels endured from their own subordinates. Those who dare not criticize the phenomenon call it "the spirit of the Army"; others give it nastier names, such as "insubordination," "fascism," and others. Whatever the name assigned to it, we recognize several original features, though less numerous than they seem at first, and there is some interest in comparing this mechanism with what is happening in civilian circles, for it has been a long time since any minister or delegate-general in France, or no doubt elsewhere,[4] was ignorant enough to presume that he commanded. The Army is only a fragment of the nation—neither an ultra-nation nor an anti-nation—and the currents of thought which nourish or disperse us also circulate within this body that makes up a part of ourselves.

Nevertheless, the marks of the cruel division that mutilated France from 1940 to 1945 subsist in our army more than anywhere else. There are still many officers whom chance placed on the wrong side—and

---

[4] A cartoon from the Washington *Post* in 1959 shows a tiny Eisenhower speaking to a huge De Gaulle and asking him his impressions "when you *really* govern." In France, the opposition papers daily printed cartoons showing the reverse situation.

who thereby not only consider themselves ruined in terms of their career but still suffer from a degree of separation from the profound current of our national life. Moreover, during the last fifteen years, the Army, unthinkingly engaged in wars contrary to the real interests of France, fought in distant lands. Each man who landed there immediately breathed in the gusts of a hostility he could not yet have produced and whose origin he did not analyze. Hatred—whatever one does—tarnishes any metal.

When struggling and suffering are an obvious necessity, this obviousness is a kind of comfort to men of spirit. In Indochina, the French Army suffered greatly, without having such comfort; France was indifferent to this war. But the young men who died in the jungles were, for their part, obliged to find it "interesting."

I learned recently, not without indignation (and I checked the facts, so incredible did they seem to me), that during the war in Indochina the blood banks in several French cities, notably Lyon, guaranteed prospective donors that their blood would not be used for military purposes.[5]

---

[5] Among its best qualities, the Communist party cultivates a sense of the public good; it is a fact that the blood donors are, in large numbers, Communist workers. The party took a strong position against the Indochinese war, since our enemy was directly supported by Moscow. Certain hospital centers, in order to keep the number of workers who furnished them

To refuse blood to a wounded enemy corrupts a sacred pact with life—it is degrading. But the nation that refuses its blood to its own soldiers corrupts itself and them. It exposes them; it exposes itself.

In January 1957, politicians of the Left entrusted these same soldiers with exorbitant powers. Of course, one must judge severely the excesses of which certain military elements then became guilty, but even more severely those men who encouraged these elements to commit such excesses and who had every opportunity to know that these cruelties were *avoidable* and that they should have been avoided at any cost.

Misery and danger endured in common in a hostile environment normally develops a certain virtue, which Ibn Khaldoun calls *aacebiya*, a word roughly translated by "esprit de corps."

This virtue consists in supporting our battle companions as if they were our brothers, whatever they do and even when we disapprove of them. Twenty years of uninterrupted fighting in great moral solitude have worked this feeling to the pitch of paroxysm throughout the entire French Army, and this powerful feeling, which, again according to Ibn Khaldoun, is the cement of state, would inevitably turn against the state

---

with blood from considerably diminishing, therefore posted this shameful exclusion.

In Algeria, France was fighting mere nationalists, who were, on several occasions, opposed to the French Communists; consequently, the two wars provoked different popular reactions.

itself—unless the state agreed to continue indefinitely the absurd struggles whose only sure finality would be the destruction of every French position.

France outside of France

During this time, outside of France, the new conditions of human life favored among all subject peoples an awareness of the constraints they endured, of their original existence, of their increasing numerical strength, and of the many and various supports the complexity of world politics offered them. Inevitably they would try to free themselves from any trusteeship and would certainly succeed in doing so.

Until the forests of Gaul were cleared, our ancestors were either "savages" or "colonized peoples." They ceased being so a little over a thousand years ago, and France began to play her starring role in the history of the planet that is our chief concern.

Today, after some ten centuries, the relative importance of our country is gradually lessening, not because her values have weakened or her energy failed, but on account of the stupendous giant nations.

Normally, we should cease to inspire fear. In the age of multitudes, inspiring fear does not present only advantages, and we see that even those who have the means to inspire fear are making great efforts to seduce. Moreover, every position presents aspects in which the disadvantages and the favors of destiny are mingled, and policy (a good policy, I mean) consists in neutralizing the former and utilizing the latter.

We no longer alarm the really powerful nations, while representing in their eyes a considerable balance in the scale of power—two reasons that have earned us a good deal of circumspect treatment from them. The more appreciable this balance, the stronger our position will be.

Confronting the new states, however, the two "super-states" are hampered by their very power, and their generosities alarm governments which, barely emerging from trusteeship, obviously fear that hands so obligingly stretched out to them may close over their wrists. They are not mistaken, for it is dangerous to frequent those stronger than oneself, and power is a temptation which some great men may resist but which inevitably triumphs over great states.

Yet these young nations must live; they want to live. In order to do so, they must catch up with a technological lead which is initially enormous and which widens daily.

Their languages do not lend themselves to instruction in the sciences. Of course, they can be adapted, but this means an additional delay, which in this dangerous race can be fatal. Life is not waiting. It demands doctors, engineers, scientists, and inventors—immediately.

To produce them quickly, right away, they seek a language of widespread use, solidly established on every continent, supported by a nation rich and populous enough to maintain it at the peak of scientific interest, invention, fashion; they seek a civilization from which no man feels excluded, *but, more than that, they seek a nation which does not threaten them, directly or indirectly.*

Now, I believe that France is tired of playing the bogeyman, and I believe she possesses all that the peoples of Africa are seeking: the rich language, well established in every latitude, a civilization open to the future, the vitality necessary for the creative ferment to continue.

She possesses not only this but a master trump as well—Paris: that strange phenomenon, the most international of cities, which despite the freakish policy we have been pursuing these last fifteen years, imperturbably increases the intensity of the currents that bind her to the universe.

"Paris-ma-grand'-ville"

Whereas France finds herself outdistanced by giants unknown to the foregoing centuries, Paris remains a capital of the world.

Other cities juxtapose interminable rows of houses and, in the nights of the planet Earth, gleam with all

their millions of volts. But that is not enough to become that strange site where values no longer accumulate, but multiply.

All these roofs rolling to the horizon, broken by the
straight furrows of the streets, are only the appearance
of this magical site, creator of civilization, where human invention meets its best opportunities, on condition that it concentrates, attracts, and absorbs everything that approaches, only to explode and overflow.
Confronting this gigantic effervescence, one thinks of
the boiling of the elemental seas, and of the billions of
sterile chemical reactions that preceded a few privileged reactions in which life appeared.

Here the miracle demands a fortunate situation
favored by history—preliminary conditions that many
capitals fulfill. Yet for one of them to attain the peak
of its destiny it must also be the beating heart of a
large, rich nation with a strong national feeling, which
sacrifices everything to it and receives everything from
it, in an incessant exchange by which everyone is enriched.

And confronting this electrode, so heavily charged
with a determined current, there must be another electrode, charged with a powerful and contrary current—
international, extranational, so to speak. Foreign, in
any case.

A "capital of the world" must be both the most
national of cities, the point of convergence of the en-

tire living genius of a great people, who are irresistibly
lured to it—and also the most international of cities,
the one where travelers, men without a country, all
the nostalgic lonely people of the world, feel more at
home than anywhere else, the city where the exotic
currents of the earth meet, carrying in chaotic bulk
the alien and the remote. The great chemical reactions
we call progress are bought at this price.

I have seen New York and London, and I love
them; one feels there that electric, gigantic air crack-
ling with discoveries everywhere; Moscow benefits
from a similar privilege. But England has given less to
her city than France to her Paris: England, for instance, witholds her finest universities for herself; Russia establishes her writers in the country, we are told;
and the United States offsets an excessive centralization by maintaining a federal structure suited to the
dimensions of its territory.

For these good reasons, among the four major capital cities—Paris, New York, London, Moscow, *un-
divided properties which a nation shares, and must
share, with all the rest*—Paris remains, Paris maintains
and multiplies, an unrivaled power of fascination.

It is true that, in its converging and centrifugal
forces, the rhythm of thought accelerates, intellectual
exchanges are enriched. Of course, men always possess
the same individual value, but this value is revealed,
like that of a light bulb, when the current passes

through it. One soon grows accustomed to this self-enrichment, to the *air de Paris*—as to the smell of coffee—until one can no longer live without it, and, the world over, men who have known it endure their separation from it as an exile.

"*Paris-la-grand'-ville*" increasingly overflows its national basis, and the French occasionally complain of this exuberance, which upsets them and which, quite directly, lies at the source of their disorders; but it engenders and maintains, too, their rarest privileges, in a quite inextricable combination, forbidding them to modify what irritates them, in consideration of what aids them. Moreover, disequilibrium and exuberance depend on them less than they think.

The Men of the Marches

SINCE THE First World War, in the hexagon of France —that crucible where our essential phenomena occur —Paris, the gigantic mixer, accelerated its abrasion of our regional peculiarities, and as its panting rhythm spread to the barbwire of our frontiers, what Balzac, Stendhal, and our parents used to call the provinces grudgingly sought refuge in literature.

Deep in the fast-beating heart of our community, the means of living and thinking are created and abandoned in such quantity that a process of selection rules; little is retained, and only what pleases.

Once one leaves our vital center, the pulsations grow weaker and the encroachments of alien cultures increase; then the instinct for survival obliges us to preserve not only what is useful or beautiful but anything at all. In every civilization the same principle operates, and inhabitants of border regions—the "men of the marches"—are necessarily both somewhat exotic and somewhat superannuated—superannuated because they are reluctant to accept the "exoticism." This permits them to claim their birthrights. They do not fail to do so.

Their country fades all the same. It disappears first, and without anyone's noticing, from institutions—then from ways of behaving, and thinking.

South of the Mediterranean, among our colonial émigrés—as in Quebec, in Liège—the *air de Paris* no longer arrives save by request, in sealed bottles, for the exclusive use of connoisseurs. *Now, such connoisseurs do not necessarily belong to the French minority, for Paris is an international phenomenon.*

Some descendants of the Algerian *colons* have no difficulty adapting themselves to this remoteness, this inevitable blurring; like many Canadians, Swiss, and Belgians, they love France and can easily criticize the French. On the other hand, they have great difficulty adapting themselves to a more painful analogy: like the Canadians under English (and now American) pressure, like the Belgians confronted by Germanism (and now by Europe), the French islets of North Africa can no longer postpone the attempt to find a viable equilibrium with Africa, with Islam. Unfortunately, everything has been done to help them postpone the fatal encounter. Everything—licit and illicit alike.

But the longer an inevitable encounter is postponed

—and this is certainly true of the Algerian encounter—
the more ruinous and redoubtable it becomes.

Dominant minorities

In Algeria, the fact we must never lose sight of—for
it is the basis of yesterday's and today's catastrophes—
derives from the coexistence of two populations with
vigorous, radically distinct "personalities."

They are inextricably mingled, and in a very dangerous proportion: more than nine million Africans on
one side, one million Europeans on the other.

The enormous gap is widening; in twenty years the
minority will be only a twentieth of the majority. *And
then only if a* modus vivendi *exists and is found.*

Today's world, like yesterday's, abounds in minorities that suffer persecution, and men of spirit interested in helping them have their work cut out for
them; on the other hand, majorities subject to the oppression of a minority are becoming increasingly rare.

By 1954, the Middle East and all of Asia had already escaped European control; in 1955 it was Tunisia and Morocco, and then, in a chain reaction, all
the other African states, with the exception of South
Africa, where the white community still persecutes a
native population four times more numerous than its
oppressors; Kenya, where sixty thousand Englishmen
confront six million Africans—one to a hundred; and

finally Algeria, where a million privileged whites desperately defend these privileges against a majority ten times their number.

A glance at these figures shows us France's responsibility in this conflict, for the struggle would have been settled—one way or another—long since if the power of our country, the proximity of its frontiers, and the almost unconditional support it has given the minority for over a century had not permitted the imbalance to be maintained beyond any normal possibility.

In order for a minority and a majority living together for generations to continue to remain distinct, a religious frontier or violent racist sentiments must oppose the mixture; normally, the minorities are absorbed by the majorities.

This "stabilized disequilibrium" has a name: it is called colonialism—a word greatly misunderstood (naturally) in the countries that have not experienced it.

Colonialism

During the period that followed the 1830 landing, Algerians and French fought, on the whole, as equals. On each side, a relatively small military force wielded sabers and rifles of equivalent power.

Nineteen centuries before, in the battles between Vercingetorix and Caesar, our own ancestors had the similar advantage of the terrain and also an armament which, archaeology tells us, was slightly superior to Rome's. Were they, then, less bellicose than the ancestors of the Italians? Neither less nor more, probably. Yet they were conquered—by a solid and stable organization called a state.

After the armed expeditions, the colonizations begin: foreigners settle in the country that arms have opened to them, trying to *adapt it to themselves*—and not to adapt themselves to it—which constitutes a second violence, more durable than the preceding one.

The minority which benefits—*to its misfortune*— from such an inversion of power in Algeria is descended from families who emigrated from France, Italy, Spain, Malta, and settled in the Algerian countryside after the French conquest of 1830 in order to till the soil.

For 130 years they have proliferated and, unlike what has happened in Tunisia and Morocco, almost all their descendants, because of unfavorable economic conditions, have abandoned agriculture to become city dwellers—often rather poor city dwellers. They live today in big cities and small ones and, *as much as possible, keep to themselves.*

This abandonment of the countryside by the Frenchmen of Algeria produced a hiatus in their assimilation by the Algerian earth. This was followed, inevitably, by a reaction, for in these relations among peoples—essentially effective—immobility is unknown.

In Morocco and Tunisia, the European *colons*, arriving later and provided with much larger holdings, as well as capital sufficient to exploit them, generally managed to maintain themselves there until the independence of these two countries.

Political—and not economic—difficulties now force them to leave. At the moment of the crisis, their dispersion among the native people kept the *colons* from even thinking of turning against them. And this was a great advantage for everyone, including the *colons*.[1]

In Algeria, on the contrary, the compact regrouping of the Europeans in cities favors the birth of a distinct "public opinion," and the presence of the surrounding Moslem masses maintains in these urban crowds a combative anxiety that has long induced them to organize their society defensively.

---

[1] Many French *colons* in Tunisia have been induced to leave the country during the last three years, not without understandable bitterness. It is nonetheless true that all the French in Tunisia declare that *even in the periods of great tension* (particularly the Sakhiet period) they suffered no moment of anxiety for their lives and those of their families. In Morocco there was an extremely bloody crisis at Meknes after the inspection of a plane carrying F.L.N. leaders, but this was brief and localized. From this moment on, the behavior of the Moroccan population toward the French has been increasingly more friendly than the experiences of the political actuality lead one to think.

The all-powerful *colons* of Algeria, mourning the victims of terrorism, no doubt envy the lot of the French in Tunisia.

The leaders of this minority, provided with considerable sums and solidly supported by turbulent groups, had already succeeded, under the Third Republic, in manipulating the Paris government, using methods that were constantly being improved toward this end.

Among the privileges the minority enjoyed and of which the majority was deprived, one of the most decisive was, for a long time, that of education.

Access to schools and universities has always been available, in France, to children of all origins, but for a child to be able to go to a *lycée* and then to a university he must first have attended primary classes for eight years—in other words, it is essential that his school be no more than about three miles from his home.

Schools were built in all the Algerian villages and cities where the European minority lived, whereas in the countryside where the Moslem farmers and shepherds lived, no schools—or virtually none—were built. Many of our compatriots have exposed this injustice, in particular the late Albert Camus. In short, today in Algeria, a thirty-year-old Moslem has had virtually a hundreds times less chance than a European his age of attaining the *baccalauréat* level [2] and fifteen times less

---

[2] In 1954, men of European origin between the ages of twenty and fifty numbered approximately 200,000; Moslem men of the same age were precisely eight times more numerous (in the under-twenty group the Moslems were thirteen times more numerous than children and adolescents of the

opportunity of attaining the level of the *certificat d'études*.

This initial privilege of education permitted the descendants of the *colons* to eliminate, in almost every administrative post of Algeria, the officials directly sent from metropolitan France and trained there. Between 1900 and 1950, France was an expanding nation, and offered more opportunities to immigrants than to her impoverished and subsequently decimated generations.

For over a century "French Algeria," the Algeria of the *colons*—following the example of the American colonists—continually and deliberately enlarged the distance between France and the new country it wished to create for its exclusive benefit.

Yet our national presence continued to affirm itself in the Maghreb by symbols—the language, the flag, the uniforms—while the gap widened once you crossed the Mediterranean. The same subtle effect obtains when you leave France for Wallonia, Lausanne, or the province of Quebec.

---

same age belonging to the French minority). In the European group, 180,000 men had attended primary school and 30,000 had attended secondary school; in the Moslem group (eight times more numerous), 100,000 had attended primary school and 3,000 had attended secondary school. Since 1955 an enormous effort has been made by the French educational system to remedy this situation, and by October 1960 a million Algerian children were going to school.

This gap derives from institutions different from our own, different in form and in spirit.[3] It derives still more from an administration recruited on the spot, which has developed in a closed milieu, influenced by a context alien to us.

I have spent time in Switzerland, in Belgium, in Canada, in the French circles of North Africa, and have tried to analyze the quality common to them all: an odor of France that is a little faded, that smells of closets, of museums, of mothballs, but in which you can still recognize a stubborn smell over all the powerful aromas of America, Africa, Germania.

In these three borderlands—not of our language, which continues far beyond them, but of our national "personality"—the confrontation is a severe one. On either side something is won, something lost; but by a strange phenomenon we lose where we thought to gain, and often gain what we had agreed to lose.

A distant France

Some of the ordeals endured by the colonized peoples are readily understood by anyone—for instance, the appropriation of land by the conqueror. Then come the legislative and administrative privileges the conqueror arrogates to himself, with their conse-

---

[3] It is generally unknown in France that before 1954 a very large number of French laws were not applicable in Algeria.

quences: that inflection of justice which corrodes the *colon* as much as the colonized.

All this disgusts the honest men who learn of it, wherever they are, whatever their condition. On the other hand, another series of ordeals, and more cruel ones—the ones that consist in imposing on a people an alien civilization—generally escape the attention of those who have not endured such trials themselves. Not only does this violence escape them but they often take it, in good faith, for a blessing.

Before continuing, let us try to examine this distant France whose edges fray and are frayed, which impregnates and is impregnated, which blurs and runs. And thereby we may come to a better understanding of that Arabism which opposes it and which, on its margins, also blurs and frays.

To understand the callosities forming where two vigorous and original civilizations overlap, I chose Canada, a pacified country—for one still sees there the scars of the struggle that for over two centuries drained the French peasants "colonized" by a nation (today our friend) which does not speak their language or share their religion.

I am well aware that the old dispute has lost all its echoes in Europe. Frenchmen have survived two wars in which the English were their allies through thick and thin; even our young men remember the radio, hidden in the most soundproof room, that brought the voices from London every night; nor do we forget the R.A.F. planes, and the risks they took to strike the enemy without harming our people.

Extremely conservative, the diplomats and the secret services of our two nations continue to deceive each other—over oil, the zone of free exchange, or the Middle East—but when either of these systems goes too far, it provokes equally virulent censure from either nation's public opinion. The rest of the time, the English and the French pay little attention to the quibbles of their Foreign Office and our Quai d'Orsay.

In Canada, the venerable quarrel still survives. It no longer causes bloodshed, of course, but on invisible frontiers irritation and reserve have replaced ambush and raids.

For a Frenchman who thinks he knows his country, a stay in the province of Quebec is a moving, and disconcerting, experience.

If he closes his eyes, he hears an old peasant speech full of those savory words severe grammarians have pruned from our own language; he never knew these tales, these songs, these proverbs, and yet he recognizes them, so easy is the phrase, the melody—easy for him— and they readily find in his memory a resting place tenderly prepared by his own childhood.

Yet, once he opens his eyes, the things he sees look alien, unaccustomed, and offensively ugly. The village itself with its anonymous wooden houses painted in garish colors, lacking any old or fine monument, suggests, from a distance, a package of candy spilled out on a monotonous carpet—too green in summer, too white in winter. The magic charm of the old poems vanishes abruptly—"La Belle dans les prisons d'amour," "Marian-son dame jolie," "P'tit Roi de France," "Blanche biche". . . . Now we are in the marches of the American civilization, but we must look elsewhere for the magnificent products of that civilization, in New York, Hollywood, even Montreal. Not here.

Here the furniture is new, sketchy, temporary. The can of condensed milk, open on a corner of the table, will in a moment add its calories to those of the black brew steaming on the stove; there will be plenty of butter and bread too, but—like the oil—they are tasteless. Despite the warm clothes, the solid shoes, we are among poor people here—privileged poor people, for they have a future of prosperity, but poor people marked by the spoliations, the frustrations, the humiliations of the past, and marked so deeply that the ravages still show.

Ravaged peoples

In Canada pure violence is an old story; it goes back two centuries. It includes odious episodes, such as the deportation of the Acadians, during which, in 1755, the British governor, Lawrence, removed all the in-

habitants of the province and abandoned them on a
deserted coast surrounded by pitiless virgin forests,
where most of them died. Two thousand French
Acadians were able to escape, and the governor hunted
them down, paying twenty to thirty pounds for each
prisoner, "Acadian or savage, dead or alive."

After the century of violence came the century of
secret and indirect oppression; it, too, ended long ago—
with the birth of the Canadian Confederation[4] in
1867.

Since that time, a true peace has prevailed, orderly
and prosperous. It has been accompanied by the realities of independence: in 1908, the last British troops
were withdrawn from Canada, which then ensured its
own defense, and no Imperial treaty can involve the
Dominion without its explicit consent.

Four generations of peace—and the scars still show.
Isn't this already enough to make us stop and think?

If the French-speaking Canadians became a majority, they would not separate themselves from their
English-speaking compatriots, to whom economic
necessities bind them, but many think they would

---

[4] Each of the ten provinces of Canada possesses a government
responsible to the provincial parliament. The federal government has more extensive powers than that of the United
States; it can, in particular, reject during the period of a year
the provincial laws judged unconstitutional or contrary to the
common interest. It also has fiscal powers and annually returns
to the provinces a share of the taxes it collects.

free themselves from the British trusteeship—though it is much less of a burden than the weight of the neighboring American colossus. If they were to dissociate themselves from the British, the cruel Governor Lawrence would turn over in his grave, for he had struck his blows in the name of the unity of the British kingdom.

It will be remembered that the Canada of Cartier and Champlain was definitively cut off from France by the British conquest of 1760, sanctioned by the treaty of 1763—exactly two centuries ago.

During the first century, relations between the French peasants of Canada and their mother country were virtually non-existent. When France and England stopped fighting, relations could have been re-established, but family ties were thereafter broken and the distance between France and Canada was great for these people, most of whom had remained poor peasants.

In a representative group of songs, collected, some ten years ago, by a single author,[5] there occur more than a thousand (1,147) imported from France and less than a hundred (exactly 83) composed in Canada.

It seems as if the brutal separation from the heart of the French world had produced an immediate and lasting exhaustion of popular invention. By a necessary

[5] Carmen Roy; see the following note. The collection was made between 1948 and 1953.

vital—and *universal*—compensation, the sons dispossessed of their heritage then cling closer to each of the crumbs that can no longer be snatched from them.

Consequently, among these men who for over two centuries have lived exclusively on lumbering and a little seasonal fishing, who have never seen shepherds, do not drink wine or perform military service, we find, among these thousand songs they have so piously preserved in their memory, 75 shepherd's songs, 143 drinking songs, 111 soldier's songs, 83 sailor's songs.

"Forty-three songs are set in Paris, ten in London, six in Orléans, four in Nantes, three in Quebec, two in Ottawa, and two in Montreal. The countries mentioned are: France (36 times), 'les îles' (22 times), Spain (18 times), Canada (10 times), America (8 times), Italy (7 times), England (6 times), Alsace and the Gaspé (5 times), Martinique, Africa, and Russia (4 times), the Netherlands and St. Helena (3 times) . . ." [6]

We might note that Russia and St. Helena have reached their place in the popular geography of the Gaspé lumberjacks by the paths of history—like the baggage of the Great Emperor. Alsace, too, crossed

---

[6] Carmen Roy: *Littérature orale en Gaspésie* (Ottawa: National Museum of Canada, 1955), p. 247. The National Museum of Canada has recorded about 12,000 French versions, corresponding (according to Luc Lacourcière) to 3,000 original old songs. In this tremendous collection, the percentage of songs of Canadian origin is still less than that indicated by the author we have just quoted.

the Atlantic only after 1871, with "L'Oiseau qui vient de France."

During the summer of 1954, touring the Gaspé Peninsula by the single road that follows the sea-coast, I occasionally saw a few modest cottages which, isolated as they were, displayed the tricolor. No particular reason for this, I was told, no holiday or ceremony; the houses were inhabited by Canadians of old stock and it was simply an ordinary affirmation, an everyday affair. A strange affirmation, in this country so completely cut off from us in the days of the *fleurs-de-lis*; it can be explained only by that kind of stubbornness one finds in certain adults who in childhood suffered intolerable constraint. The constraint is over, of course, and long ago. But the sores still remain.

During this long and observant trip, friends took me to visit the local celebrities in each village—storytellers, singers, bonesetters, healers. Following worn paths, we reached wooden houses without electricity, where the ancient inhabitants were most often illiterate. They explained that the nearest doctor lived far away, that in their childhood he had been virtually inaccessible, that many of them still followed the customs of their ancestors—curing their heart ailments with infusions of porcupine quills and their bronchitis with the milk of a black mare. "When a child has mumps," they said, "you rub his neck against the pig's trough."

In France, I always listen to old country people's conversations; I like hearing about the price of wheat, ghost stories, the election of the municipal council. Listening, I sometimes try to date words and customs, eager to find the old stone under the century's alluvium. In the house of this old northern Gaspé lumberjack, the rural seventeeth century—which Marc Bloch called *terra incognita*—speaks to us directly.

My host, great-grandson of a Malouin, could neither read nor write, but his infallible memory constituted an almost inexhaustible repertoire of popular knowledge.[7] He had medical talents; he cured warts, and stopped hemorrhages by spells.

His stories delighted me. In them, one lives deep in a strange forest. Is this the Gallic *sylva* where his ancestors and mine, ten centuries ago, killed wolves, cut roads, and pulled old stumps to make their fields? Is this the impenetrable green cloak of the New World which his ancestors rediscovered two hundred years ago—wild, deserted, with no trails but those of the caribou, the bears, and the elk? The elk, on the carpets of moss under the birches, now meets the Wizard Merlin, Jean de l'Ours, and Hop o' My Thumb.

His repertoire was learned by heart; he revised it mentally, improved it, added to it, and recited it with

---

[7] He could sing 330 songs and tell 70 tales (most of which were longer than a novel) without exhausting his repertoire.

undiscriminating respect and priestly dignity. Between "Les Ecoliers de Pontoise," a song that, I believe, dates back to the reign of Louis XI, and "Roy Renaud," whose first-known prototype is a Nordic saga, he sang the "Marseillaise" as he had learned it:

> *Je suis l'enfant de la Patrie*
> *Le jour de gloire est arrivé.*
> *Entre nous et l'Arbanie*
> *Nous irons tous deux promener . . .*

In another home, I found a snow-bearded patriarch, an old fisherman from the southern part of the province.

While one of his daughters-in-law tried, at my request, to count his children, grandchildren, and great-grandchildren, the head of the family (who had seventeen sons and daughters, all living) sang me some of his repertoire, including an endless ballad of the misfortunes of the Grande Armée during the retreat from Russia.

Astonished, I asked the old bard if he knew other songs on the same subject. Yes, he knew more. And without any apparent fatigue, he sang them for hours on end. Napoleon, always the central character,[8] was either an odious tyrant or an ideal hero, and the old

---

[8] In one Canadian tale, Napoleon is represented as waging war on the Indians in the forests of the New World (Luc Lacourcière Collection, Laval University, Quebec).

man sang with all his heart and his best effects for either the regrets of the Napoleonic *grognards* or the sarcasms of the *ci-devants*. I myself love our old songs and collect them, and I realized that all of his were new to me.

During the First Empire, French Canada was totally cut off from France—morally, for the Canadians remained legitimists; materially, for they were no less suspect in the eyes of the British government, which observed them closely and patrolled all coastal waters.

Is it not impressive that, under such conditions, these delicate flowers should have traversed thousands of miles and hundreds of years? Invisible and weightless, they passed customs and frontiers, in the wretched luggage of the emigrants; they crossed the Atlantic, paddled upstream in birch-bark canoes, strode along the new continent's paths. Having finally reached these forsaken hamlets, the poor lumberjacks and illiterate fisherman—without the help of a book, a newspaper, or a school—with effort, with patience, for six generations reverently handed them on.

In France, for several generations, the book alone has inspired confidence. The spoken word and memory have become its auxiliaries—secondary tools, and rather suspect. It is no longer France that this application, this religious solemnity, reminds me of now.

In Algeria, as in Canada, you can find poor French

peasants, yet it is not of them either that I am thinking now, for these little *colons* of the department of
Constantine, whose grandparents emigrated a generation or two after the sailors from Saint-Malo, forebears
of the old Canadian bard, had schools and the unconditional support of a powerful administration. No,
this diligent tone, this affecting seriousness, I have seen
among the old men of the Maghreb, in the *amoqran*
and the *taleb*.[9] They, too, alone against the opposing
flood, stateless, without schools, virtually without
books, maintain what they have left of an august tra-
dition and confuse in the same devotion all it has
bequeathed to them, shapeless pebbles and gold dust.

The foolish mockery that is occasionally directed at
both groups makes me blush, and I would like the
pedants who make fun of them to come here and see
what becomes of one of the proudest civilizations when
it ceases to be maintained by the rigid armature of a
state. A mild punishment. They will have their sick
ears rubbed against the pig's trough.[1]

---

[9] *Amoqran*: a Berber word meaning "great," "old man," and
referring to the men who speak in the tribal council. *Taleb*:
an Arab word for the itinerant scholars who teach the Koran
to young children.
[1] This custom seems to have vanished from Brittany, where it
was still observed at the end of the nineteenth century. The
Breton peasants explained it as follows: "We noticed that
pigs, who are very subject to mumps, cure themselves by rub-

The pieds noirs[2]

The expansion of the Europeans who emigrated to Algeria cannot be compared with the vigor of the Canadian expansion, but it offers one analogy: the determining influence of the first population and the ease with which it absorbs the newcomers.

How often I have heard people insist, with many figures and details, that the Perezes and the Pietris of the Maghreb are Italians, Spaniards, Maltese, and not Frenchmen as they claim. As often, at least, as I have heard harsh speeches about the Berbers of Algeria and their absurd claims to Arabism. But the Berbers who want to be Arabs *are* Arabs, and the Maltese who want to be Frenchmen *are* Frenchmen. And their children all the more.

In Canada, it is easy to demonstrate the determining influence of the initial amalgam. The first French colonists, who landed there in 1604, numbered only

---

bing their ears and neck against the trough of the sty." Before jeering, we might note that Jenner devised the anti-variola vaccination, around 1776, after noticing the immunity acquired by the cowherds when they had occasion to milk cows afflicted with the disease called "vaccinia."

[2] The Frenchmen of Algeria have given themselves this name of *pieds noirs*, "black feet." The expression may have been borrowed from the naval vocabulary, where it refers to the stokers who walk about in the coal, as opposed to the mechanics, who are called "greasy rags."

a few dozen. They called their new country Acadia and their first capital Port-Royal. In 1660 they numbered 2,000; in 1700, 16,000. Now, we know that between 1608 and 1700 only 3,757 emigrants set sail for the New World (which was already producing its own children). In 1763, when French Canada was ceded to England, the French colonists in America numbered 65,000. Between 1700 and 1763, only 5,000 emigrants had left the mother country.

We must count in these figures an average of twenty-four women a year arriving between 1634 and 1674; an average of nine women a year between 1674 and 1700. In the next century, without any doubt, the average of the female exodus fell still lower—particularly since in many cases it was not voluntary.

In short, less than 3,000 Manon Lescauts left France to become the forebears of the more than four million present-day French Canadians—to which it is convenient to add a million and a half or two million American citizens whose ancestors came from French Canada; in all, a good six million descendants.

If we keep all these figures in mind, it is easy to explain why the philologists note resemblances between Canadian French and the dialects spoken in the seventeenth (and not the eighteenth) century in Normandy, Maine, and Perche. *It is between 1634 and 1674 that the linguistic determination of French Canada occurred.*

By 1674, the twenty-four women a year[3] sent during the preceding half century by the King had produced a society. In this society, it happened, the Norman element was dominant. Constantly "deranged"[4] and disturbed by war and the ups and downs of an unstable economy, it now acquired a homogeneity within which, from 1674, all the new arrivals melted like butter.

I should like to see a parallel study made on the language of the Frenchmen of Algeria and on the places of origin of the first wave of *colons*. To the ear, it sounds as though they came from the hills of the Massif Central.

Whatever the case, there exists today in Algeria a vigorous, expansive, original European milieu, with recognizable local accents, manners, character traits, and characteristic gesticulation. The French determination of this milieu certainly dates back to its origins; it is previous to 1870.

The local people readily distinguish the Bône, Oran, Constantine, and Algiers accents, but for the Frenchmen of France (who are there called *Francaoui* or

---

[3] Gustave Lanctôt: *Filles de joie ou filles du Roy* (Montreal: Chantecler, 1952). Père Archange Godbout: *Nos Hérédités provinciales françaises* (Quebec: Archives de folklore, 1946).
[4] The Canadians called the cruel deportation of the Acadians *le grand dérangement*.

Patos[5]), all sound alike and constitute a recognizable unit.

Once in contact with this unit, made homogeneous by great "derangements," economic crises, and the cities' siphoning-off process, the new immigrants from Spain, Italy, Malta, are absorbed like drops of water by the sea.[6]

From the first generation, their descendants are "French"—and there is a great injustice in denying or begrudging them this qualification if they desire it. Besides, what is a Frenchman if not a man who considers himself French?

But in Algeria, they are not the only ones; another reality has developed near them, before them, faster, stronger . . .

---

[5] These terms are pejorative; the man from France is usually considered a fool by his Algerian compatriots. The word *Francaoui* merely means "Frenchman of France"; the word *Patos* is Spanish and means "duck."

[6] Those from France too, particularly the governors-general and the other officials Paris sends in hopes of being represented on the spot.

III

"They" Here, "We" There

DISMAYED, fascinated, the descendants of the European émigrés were aware, long before the statisticians,[1] of the growth of the young Moslem colossus—a growth in numbers and in value.

In 1938, after four years of ethnographic studies, during which I shared the life of the nomad peasants of the southern Aurès—before undertaking a third and later a fourth scientific mission in their territory—I tried, I remember, to make a record of the contacts between our civilization and theirs. This stocktaking may help us today as a reference point in measuring the road we have covered since.

---

[1] Forecasts based on statistical investigation show the annual increase of births over deaths in Algeria as follows:

1950:	220,000
1955:	260,000
1960:	310,000
1965:	360,000
1970:	420,000
1975:	490,000

In that faraway year 1938, the transformation produced by the direct relations of our civilization with the Algerian civilization was of remarkable insignificance. Today, in this area, the change reaches proportions that we do not suspect; by her schools and still more by the great waves of labor emigration, France has suddenly penetrated into the intimate lives of the Algerian people—a gigantic catalysis that has intensified and accelerated awareness.

This was not true twenty years ago. In those days, you had to look hard to discern the first traces of an infiltration, particularly in the peasant society of Constantine, where I was studying.

Improvement of farming methods by contact with the *colons?* Zero.

In the department of Constantine, at least, the contrary was the case—that is, the Italian and Corsican farmers were gradually assimilated by the local population (they did not yet dare veil their women, but they wanted to).

On the other hand, a few Kabyl workers returned from France, nostalgic and disoriented, but they kept silent or hurried back. A few teachers—the results of the diligence, in homeopathic doses, of the great educational principles of our democracy—exerted a more direct influence. For the most part, they revealed a touching loyalty to France, but timidly advocated integration. On this account, our administration

labeled them "anti-French" and snubbed them on
every possible occasion.

A second kind of transformation, on the other hand,
seemed to me, even at that early date, to conceal an
enormous explosive potential. This was the meta-
morphosis of the entire social structure owing to the
mere numerical increase of the inhabitants.

I did not base my opinion on census figures,[2] but
only on my daily observations; each time I catalogued
the subdivisions of a tribe and tried to reconstruct its
past, I discovered a gradual shrinking of the space
occupied by a family and a parallel diminution of its
resources. I saw the apparently most rigid of structures
altering in depth; for instance, in the oral traditions
of a sedentary group, I often found traces of a fairly
recent period when it followed its herds. This is a
transformation of as great a consequence as the one
that makes a farmer into a factory laborer.

*Irresistible pressure of conflicts
and passions in a growing population*

What one does not realize reading all this in a book
—but what one feels and understands when one is able

---

[2] The annual increase of the Algerian Moslem population is
recorded as:

    1926:   9 per 1,000
    1931: 16 per 1,000

to live it—are the consequences resulting from the multiplication of men. When a population doubles, it finds the number of its conflicts, its difficulties, its problems, quadrupled, but its collective passions multiply still more quickly, inevitably rousing the people, according to circumstances, to a pitch encouraging dynamism and the spirit of enterprise—but also hostility and even outright hysteria.

Those who remember the summer of 1940, and an anemic France[3] lying supine before her invader, can compare her with that same France twenty years later, alive with young people and aspiring to international status—sometimes, unfortunately, quite inopportunely.

That some of us would have preferred our country a little more vehement in 1940, when the cruelest dangers threatened her life—and a little less splenetic

---

1936: 21 per 1,000
1954: 30 per 1,000

[3] In 1941, agonized by our defeat and trying to understand its causes, I read a great many German works on the sociology of our two nations. The author of one of these wrote that France should be attacked in 1939, the year of its greatest weakness, the year when its "active population" would be at its lowest level.

As a matter of fact, in 1939 the men who died in the preceding war (two million men *hors de combat*) would still have been of an age to hold productive posts, while the children born in 1918—the least numerous generation of the century—had just reached their majority. After 1940, our "active" curve rose again, while the children born after the bloody victory of 1918 reached man's estate.

twenty years later—changes nothing in events, nothing in the collective behavior that our will does not determine. But if such a change could have occurred, and in so short a time, in our old, lucid, and satiated country, what will happen in Africa, what will become of Algeria, *whose rhythms of growth and reasons for grudge are so much more intense than our own?*

Of course, these six years of war (a war whose cruelty France does not imagine) represent for the Algerian people a loss in human life impossible to calculate at present, but however enormous, this loss cannot dam the irresistible current represented by the multiplication of men and the super-multiplication of passions.

This enormous reserve of power could be diminished only (in independence) by the pitiless grip of poverty or (in a colonial regime) by an iron fist, the absence of schools, and a deliberate "fixing" of elections or their suppression altogether. But this entire mechanism of oppression functions only in wartime; it excludes a peaceful integration within the normal framework of a democratic France.

There are two alternatives: either France must abandon a republican regime and accept the "hair shirt" and the discipline necessary to fetter Algeria; or, if she maintains her social legislation, her educational standards, her freedom of expression, she must face the fact that she cannot indefinitely forestall osmosis between the two nations. Consequently, at a date more or less close at hand, Algeria must inevitably free herself.

Such considerations, moreover, are quite academic. The African peoples now flow toward their independence like rivers toward the sea—irresistibly.

The double Algerian advance

Between the First and Second world wars, one could already discern, in some circles, a political claim—still a legal one—and increasing individual competition— the first symptoms of modern Algeria. Already a young native elite was being established in all the liberal professions (that is, at the still uncrossed thresholds of administrative power); already a portion of this elite was obliged to emigrate.[4]

This first French-speaking "intelligentsia" included men of worth who sought a vital equilibrium for their people; they understood the views of Governor-General Violette[5] and supported his policy. His failure, and

---

[4] Thirty years ago, some thirty Algerian instructors taught French in the schools of Fès.

[5] The Blum-Violette plan specified the enfranchisement of a gradually increasing number of Algerians, in order to associate Algeria with France—at first only 21,000 Algerian Moslems. The *colons* rejected this plan that would have saved them.

Shortly before his death, M. Violette, then a deputy, confided to one of his colleagues that the memory of the attacks made against him during his authority in Algeria still woke him up at night.

the brutal and uncouth reaction that followed this honest man's departure, nipped such hopes in the bud and inspired a certain amount of emigration, but it was of the kind critically weakening for a nation: the emigration of young people who had completed their high school education.

At this stage, the phenomenon called colonialism distorts all the laws of competition, but it is so stubborn that in 1960 (and despite all the speeches, promises, orders, or circulars), it still managed to keep the majority at least partially away from posts of authority. Of course, in order to exclude that majority for so long from its own country, it had been necessary to deploy the whole arsenal of the most dishonest dodges, to violate our own laws all the time—which was an action both base and stupid—and all the more stupid in that, thanks to the French schools (France, like the man in the fable, blows hot and cold), the number of young Algerians who had completed high school was increasing every day.

At the origin of the first wave of Algerian intellectuals, one finds a few country schools with devoted French teachers, scholarships, the good principles of the Third Republic—all things regarded with extreme

---

Governor-General Châtaigneau, who fifteen years later attempted to resume the same policy, also endured a prepared campaign of threats, calumnies, and anonymous letters.

aversion by the leaders of the French minority in Algeria.

Almost simultaneously, a first mass contact occurred between Moslem Algeria and metropolitan France, following the workers' emigration into France.

The two world wars had already displaced several hundred thousand men. A great number of these received, in the Army, a training that permitted them to adapt themselves to life in Europe. The return of these men to all the social stratifications of the Algerian nation has certainly played a decisive role in the mechanism of the workers' emigrations. For a man to make a major decision (for instance, to go to a foreign country), it must first be *conceivable*, then possible, and only lastly necessary; it is military service that made their exodus conceivable to the peasants of Algeria.

The beginnings of the civilian exodus occurred before 1939. In this first phase, a few illiterate mountain tribesmen who cross the sea to try to earn their bread are virtually unnoticed. They pass through the heedless crowds, brown and furtive, selling flowers, peanuts, doing the undesirable jobs in building yards and factories—no more exotic than the coal seller from Auvergne, the little Breton *bonne*, the Italian masons, or the Polish Jews who make caps in the rue des Rosiers. The great city pulverizes, masticates, digests.

Twenty-five years later, everyone who reads his paper

knows that the *Etoile nord-africaine*[6] was created in
Paris in 1925 or 1926, in an Algerian laboring milieu;
twenty-five years later, one meets certain doctors, certain lawyers, certain professors, certain mathematicians
or chemists whose brilliant studies have been paid for
during these already long-distant years by a father or
an elder brother out of his laborer's salary. To achieve
this result, the illiterate émigré must have had to deprive himself daily of what in France we call the "vital
minimum," and even before he could do that he had
to grasp the mechanisms and the values of an alien
world, indoctrinate his family, separate his little boy
from his mother and then push him—ardently, pa-
tiently, proudly—to the fore.

After 1945 the sporadic emigration became an enormous wave—400,000 men, constantly replacing one
another. Moslem Algeria finds itself at the nexus of
two advances: first an "intellectual" elite which, to
a decisive degree, has issued directly from the prole-
tariat; second, hundreds of thousands of men, born
peasants, who have received the "training of the cities"

---

[6] Directed by M. Ahmed Messali, called Messali Hadj, who is
the leader of an Algerian nationalist movement of a small
minority, the M.N.A. (Mouvement National Algérien). Since
1955, bloody conflicts have broken out between the F.L.N.
and the M.N.A., which for a long time has maintained a certain hold among the workers in the North of France. In Algeria, the M.N.A. has lost a good deal of its credit with the
Moslem population, which by the end of 1957 accused it of
collusion with the French police and Army.

from Europe. *These two advances are unique in Africa,
and under their double influence the Algerian masses
are developing with a speed of which the Western
world has as yet no experience.*

The consequences of this stirring up, this ferment,
will begin to appear around 1980. Today we can nevertheless discern that a true social mutation occurred
when the revolution began—a secret incandescence
that sapped the old medieval structures in the silence
of a country without a voice. For almost seven years
the storm of war has blown over these coals, accelerat-
ing the disintegration of the great tortured body. Yet
it has not been destroyed; once the agony stops—then,
between the red coals, the metal will gleam forth.

On Algerian soil, a lost foreigner

The Algerian, African, Moslem reality, in all its
originality, confronted the first French *colons*. The
persistent Alsatian who drained a marsh in the Mi-
tidja, the Italian mason who spent his life building
roads in the *djebels* (sharing the life of the Arabs who
worked with him so closely and so continually that he
almost forgot his own language in speaking theirs),
were lonely foreigners. They steeped themselves in
Algeria; it penetrated them to the marrow—because a
man alone can resist a crowd no longer than a sponge
resists the sea.

Some struggled to preserve their "national personality"—struggled by regrouping in cities. Others attached themselves with all their might to this violent country. They loved its men—proud and steady, generous, courteous—and the grave landscapes: the pines, the olive trees, and the snows of Kabylia, the beaches of Oran, the *djebel* passes of the South, where suddenly the desert comes to meet you and in its light all the rest of the world is a shadow.

They planted trees, dug wells and harbors, built dikes, factories, and handsome houses covered with balconies and flowers.

In the next century, the descendants of the nostalgic émigrés (you recognize their farm, in Constantine, by a solitary ridiculous poplar beside the door) and those of the seduced conquerors are first mingled before they redistribute themselves into two enemy camps.

The sons and grandsons of the pioneers have almost all abandoned the country for the cities; now they are contractors, officials, grocers, magistrates; they speak only French and keep to themselves, gathered into compact, watertight islets—almost watertight.

Algerian society, up to 1954 or even 1955 reminds me of those old market places in our northern provinces, with their old rafters blackened by age, their huge heavy and hermetic roofs—which shelter night-flying birds of prey along with the spider webs—while underneath, the wind plays with the dead leaves and the visitors' hate.

In childhood, in adolescence even, the air still came in; Arab boys and French boys went to school together, played soccer together, fought together on the way home from school,[7] discussed everything, astonished to be so much alike. Above young heads, the shadow of superannuated institutions thickened, and the old roof pressed with the weight of all its slates on the ingenious systems of beams which time and the worms had rotted to the core.

One night in November 1954, the old roof fell in.

Was France at war with Algeria that day? Not at all. The cohabitation of the two peoples continued, and intensified; the children played together in ever greater numbers. And why shouldn't they have liked each other? Both were worthy of friendship.

I am well aware that a fiction has been circulated according to which France fought against the F.L.N. Algerians and not against the others, but any investigation made in good faith demonstrates that no frontiers exist between F.L.N. Algerians and non-F.L.N. Algerians.

---

[7] These young people had their magazines (*Conscience maghrébine, L'Espoir*) and common social enterprises; they were beginning to find out about each other, with eager curiosity. The wind of the war kindled certain friendships and extinguished others.

One day six years later, in September 1960, France suddenly realized, with astonishment, that these virtually unknown Algerians, who were waging a cruel and effective war against her, possessed in various French circles friends loyal enough to violate our laws in order to aid our adversaries, while other Frenchmen, *extremely numerous*, whom neither laws nor police can reproach, adhered by many and various and contradictory fibers to this solidarity.

But how could it be otherwise?

Had not the two peoples lived together for more than a century? Had not the children of the two peoples played together, studied together, spoken the same language, shared the bread of the body and that of the mind?

Two hundred years ago, French Protestant and Catholic children were brought up apart, were taught to hate and despise each other; in the twentieth century, our instructors no longer teach such things to our little Moslems and our little Christians.

Yet on several occasions, severe sentences have been imposed on this youth,[8] caught in the trap of our virtues, of our principles, and of the friendship that quite naturally unites young people brought up together. Some of these young Frenchmen (not all) had ex-

---

[8] Contrary to what is generally supposed, a large proportion of the Frenchmen arrested and condemned (and often tortured) for giving aid to Algerians are natives of Algeria.

ceeded the limits of the law—but the laws are sometimes in conflict with the imperatives of the oldest
human morality, notably with a very venerable and
almost universal institution, called hospitality. Moreover, the widespread use of torture inclines those who
are certain of its existence and its mechanisms to support and protect any person exposed to the possibility
of suffering it.

As for the Frenchmen who love their country, to
the very degree that they feel the solidarity that unites
them to their compatriots, they regard themselves as
responsible for the crimes committed by some among
them and ardently desire to make reparation for them
—a desire further reinforced by the natural compassion
that inclines them to correct an injustice.

As if all this—which is a great deal—were not
enough, the accidents of history would have it that
among these witnesses of the sufferings of the alien
people are certain Frenchmen who, less than twenty
years before, had directly experienced these same
crushing ordeals.

This tormented friendship is, unfortunately, reciprocal, and I know of one young *felleg* who before leaving
"on a long journey" (whose destination was not specified) visited his many French friends for the last embraces. To one of them he said: "I pray God to be
killed and not to kill."

Algeria is a country where everyone knows *every-*

thing about everyone; someone witnessed the young man's death. Then it was learned, in his shanty town, that he had joined the underground to serve as an orderly; formerly tubercular, he could not keep up with the *maquisards* and was stricken in the house of some peasants. He was captured and shot less than a month after he left.

On Paris sidewalks, a poor traveler

A hundred years after the sailing ships of the *Roy de France,* other adventurers had taken to the sea in their turn. And the new current of penetration is in the opposite direction.

Once upon a time a man of the Mediterranean named Ulysses was known to be the wisest of men. But fickle history has reversed the chronology of his adventures: the *Odyssey,* logically, should precede the *Iliad,* for the wise man is the man who knows both sides of every civilization—the wise man is first of all a poor pilgrim, before perhaps becoming a victorious warrior.

In the future, the submerged emigrant, surrounded on all sides by an unknown universe, will be that silent student who sits for the first time on a café terrace on the boulevard Saint-Michel, or that Kabyl peasant, trembling with fear and cold, who gets out of the gare de Lyon one icy March evening—the month of the Algerian famines.[9]

A century after the other conquerors, this student, this worker, are now, in their turn, to be engulfed in the great alien waves of the *other continent*. They will keep their distance, too, at first, with contempt and mistrust—then every day they will see it shrink. It will be their turn to choose a wife and a best friend, to expose to the thousand aggressions of true exile (the exile of the poor) the bundle of nonsense all the children in the world find in their cradle when they are born. It will be their turn to increase their knowledge and their wisdom—until sometimes they even understand an adversary who does not understand them—and on that account to feel, a little more often than that adversary, a certain compassion.[1]

The conquest, Père Bugeaud,[2] a hundred years of French administration, have slipped over the real

---

[9] "I'm hungry, Uncle March," says the Chaouia peasant. March answers: "What can I do for you? The old barley is gone, the new one not yet ready, but if you will wash your burnoose seven times in one day, I will dry it for you seven times."

[1] For the same reasons, a hundred years ago, things occurred in precisely the inverse fashion. In the nineteenth century, the French Army was less numerous, less controlled; many officers spoke Arabic and were able to understand and respect the Algerian rebels.

[2] Governor-general of Algeria from 1840 to 1846. *Tr. note.*

Algeria like water over a granite boulder—but here in France, for the first time, the stone splits open and the water penetrates. Explosive contact.

IV

War

SEVERAL TIMES, before and after 1945, the Paris government timidly tried to establish democracy in Algeria. Governors were appointed with this precise goal in mind; orders and formal circulars prescribed the employment of Moslems in all the jobs at the state's command. Orders, circulars, governors, careened off a glassy surface: the local administration, consisting almost entirely of the colonial population and sharing all its prejudices—exaggerating them, in fact, for it benefited directly from the appropriation of all positions.

In Algeria, in 1954, there were 113,000 employees in public or semi-public services, of whom 33,147 were Moslems; in the important jobs (Category A) there were 145 Moslems (according to an official brochure) in 1956, and 239 in August 1957. This brochure does not give the total number of officials in this category. As a matter of fact, at the end of 1958 the Algerian budget provided for 9,349 Category A positions (of which 7,394 were filled).

Insofar as this appropriation represented, in the majority's eyes, a usurpation increasingly odious because increasingly unjustified, it provoked increasing bitterness. This bitterness, perfectly well known to those who provoked it, justified and increased their chronic anxiety, their potential hostility. Nevertheless, I know officials of this administration who have systematically supported the weak and the poor, defended their goods, protected their lives—but these are men of great courage and great objectivity, and it is not reasonable to hope for such things from everyone. Ordinary men—that is, the majority—in a situation of this kind expend all their strength and ingenuity monopolizing the access to power—and when they feel threatened, they become quite disagreeable.

This new source of frustration for the Moslems alternated with the less obvious, often unformulated pain of cultural dispossession and the open exasperation provoked, among the peasants, by the confiscations of land[1]—an inexhaustible exasperation each generation transmits intact to the next. It is one that peasants the world over will understand.

In the country, the bitterness was all the sharper, for

---

[1] In the department of Constantine, from 1871 to 1878, the total amount confiscated was about 1,400,000 acres; in all of Algeria, about 12,350,000 acres.

famines grew harsher year by year because of the brutal
and excessive population increase.

And though the good land is taken, it is not taken
away: it stays where it always was, admirably culti-
vated, bearing the harvests of Canaan.

1945: the Sétif riot, a consequence of the "pacification" of 1853

Why was the demonstration organized by the
U.D.M.A. (Union Démocratique du Manifeste Algérien) on V-E Day (May 8, 1945) peaceful everywhere in Algeria save in the region of Sétif?

I have spoken of those horrible days with many and
varied witnesses. On the Moslem side, people assume
a provocation organized by the *colons*; on the *colon*
side, no one doubts the Moslem premeditation.[2]

Both views seem dubious to me, for to brew such
a plot for fifteen years—when its mechanisms are necessarily known to a great number of people—is an exploit scarcely consonant with the similarly Mediterranean temperament of either group.

On the other hand, the famine of the mountain
tribes surrounding Sétif was only too obvious, as was
the covetousness excited in them by the splendid har-

---

[2] Precise and authentic facts are cited *on both sides* to prove
enemy premeditation. Let us note that the situation was, as
people say, strained.

vests that the Compagnie genevoise de Sétif was gathering on their confiscated land (36,432 acres). Ten years later, 125 miles from here, peasants who told me about it still lost their tempers.

The Compagnie genevoise was granted the best land in the Sétif region in 1853, with no other obligation than to create ten villages of fifty hearths each. The good Swiss accountants quickly realized that such creations were burdensome and thereafter applied themselves to discouraging the European *colons* already settled there—428 in 1870, only 105 by 1923. Nevertheless, a decree issued on April 24, 1858, granted the company the ownership of the property gratis, releasing it from any obligation.[3] It subsequently sold a portion of its holdings and at a good price, but in 1944 it still possessed 36,432 acres—an insignificant part of its capital, which it may have retained inadvertently.

It would have been easy to compensate the original owners and not keep this permanently lit torch near this huge mountain of dry straw, but that would have required thought. And as ill luck would have it, Algerian Algeria didn't exist for France or for French officials.

---

[3] The Compagnie genevoise has constantly reinvested in Swiss stocks, even during the First World War. Another great company (the Compagnie algérienne) has profited from favors just as exorbitant. In 1954 it still possessed 250,000 acres.

During this period European railroad workers and postmen living in Sétif were feeling every day the hostility of the tribes around them; the tribes associated them with the great, distant bankers who, in the innocence of Switzerland, handled this dynamite only in the form of odorless dividends. The postman and the railroad worker had reasons for their fear. Fear exasperates; it exasperates the man who is afraid and the man who makes him afraid.

Repression follows the riot; nine years later insurrection follows the repression

Before 1940, I knew a number of Algerian intellectuals; those I met were militantly in favor of integration; for this reason they were assiduously persecuted by the French administration and by colonial circles who were revolted by such an insupportable claim.

Discouraged, most of them rallied to the P.P.A.[4] and to Ferhat Abbas's A.M.L.;[5] the latter was then

---

[4] Messali Hadj's *Etoile nord-africaine* was dissolved by the decree of January 25, 1937. Messali then founded a regular party, the P.P.A. (Parti du Peuple Algérien), which was proclaimed on March 11, 1937, and dissolved on September 29, 1939, after its founder was sentenced to two years' imprisonment. Condemned a second time, in 1941, to sixteen years' forced labor, Messali was freed in June 1946 by the Fourth Republic and created, in November 1946, the M.T.L.D. (Mouvement pour le Triomphe des Libertés Démocratiques).
[5] Amis du Manifeste et de la Liberté, a party founded in Sétif

advocating an Algerian Algeria federated with France.[6]

On May 8, 1945, the day of the Allied victory, a peaceful demonstration was organized by these two movements in all the cities of Algeria. It happened that Tuesday was market day in Sétif—which means that the men from the expropriated tribes were there, bitter and violent. They naturally swelled the ranks of the demonstrators who, around eight in the morning, gathered near the great mosque.

The French authorities, meanwhile, received the leaders, who promised to maintain order and disarmed their partisans themselves. Since the demonstration was not prohibited, the parade started off.

In the center of the city, on the rue de Constantine, a policeman in civilian clothes stopped the parade, brandished a revolver, and fired, killing a young boy carrying the flag.

The Moslem crowd then divided into two groups, one of which left a wreath at the monument to the war dead, while the other scattered, seized any weapons they could find, and massacred French civilians

---

on March 14, 1944, by Ferhat Abbas. After its leader's imprisonment, the A.M.L. became a regular party, the U.D.M.A., proclaimed in 1946.

[6] Between March 9 and March 15, 1960, the French Institute of Public Opinion polled men and women in all walks of life on "Algerian self-government in close union with France." This solution had sixty-four advocates out of every hundred.

at random—with stones, knives, and axes, for the demonstrators had no firearms.

Three days later, the Army began a repression that
lasted until May 16. The official account mentions
1,165 Moslem victims; the opposition press sets the
figure at 45,000 deaths. Various investigations suggest
that the actual figure must be less than 45,000 but
more than 15,000. On the European side, the dead
numbered 103 (including the 29 killed at Sétif) and
the wounded 110.

The Swiss journalist Charles-Henri Favrod,[7] in a
book filled with firsthand information, indicates the
direct influence that the 1945 repression exerted on
the 1954 revolution. This observation is completely
confirmed by all the information I myself gathered
from the witnesses of this drama. Favrod also discusses
the counterterrorist commandos who organized spon-
taneously and who on their own initiative, during a
period of several weeks, methodically assassinated innocent Algerians; there was never any attempt to punish these murderers. Finally, he refers to the direct
part played by the Algerian Communist party in the
repression;[8] it increased the mistrust the old Algerian

---

[7] *La Révolution algérienne* (Paris: Plon, 1959), p. 76.

[8] The secretary of the Communist cell in Sétif had both hands
chopped off by the rebels. The latter paraded with banners
inscribed: "Long live independent Algeria!" "Free Messali!"
"Down with colonialism!" "Down with the Communist

nationalists had shown toward this party on several
occasions (notably in 1921 and 1937).

1948: falsification of elections

In 1948 France was to suffer another great failure
in Algeria—or rather she was to permit another irreparable mistake: the systematic falsification of elections.[9]
Originally a fault, due to ignorance, absence of political forethought, weakness, the absence of civil morale.
Later on a failure, and a failure with grave consequences.

There were others, less striking, but it would be
tedious to enumerate them, for to do so would neces-
sitate following the succession of all the liberal impulses which, from Paris, attempted to reach the
crushed, offended, asphyxiated Moslem population.
Now, not only did these liberal impulses from Paris
fail but it seems, indeed, that their only effect was to
stimulate the opposition, to give it the desire—and the
occasion—for even greater rigor.

Eight years later, starting in 1956, mindless sophists
turned the apparatus of repression against what is

---

party!" (Charles-André Julien: *L'Afrique du Nord en marche*;
Paris: Payot, 1952; pp. 135 and 303).
[9] Municipal elections in 1945, 1947, and 1952; elections for
the First Constituent Assembly in 1945, for the Second Constituent Assembly in 1946, for the Algerian Assembly in April
1948.

called the O.P.A. (*organisation politico-administra-tive*), which actually designates both the youth groups formed in our schools and the traditional groups, the men people listen to in the villages. These men also knew how to talk to the F.L.N. military leaders carrying on their guerrilla warfare in the sector. It did the soldiers no harm to be reprimanded occasionally by "intellectuals" or by experienced grandfathers who preached reason and moderation.

All these local intellectuals, these pious and poor dignitaries whom an occasional year in a Billancourt factory permitted to subsist, these originals, both real aristocrats and real proletarians, were not "obedient," and it is true that they compromised with the underground, but not without receiving compromises as well.

Conversely, they neither accepted nor rejected a priori all the French initiatives; when they considered them advantageous and reasonable, they examined them, adapted them, and imposed them.

One can lean only on what resists one's weight. We saw this after 1958, when all the upper echelons of the French administration and even a few military leaders began to show solicitude over the fruits of three or four Algerian elections: "All right, a favor now, say *no* to me . . ." Unfortunately, it took more than two years to obtain this, even among the most docile.

This point had not yet been reached when, on November 1, 1954, the first shots of an interminable battle rang out.

At this date, if the Paris government had been sufficiently stable, organized, and energetic to hold really free elections in Algeria, it would have probably spared us a long and cruel war—for the interest of France, *the only interest of France in Algeria, is not to maintain herself there by force, it is to have peace, to have peace there.* This is much more difficult than to maintain herself there.

The war that dares not tell its name

At three in the morning, on November 1, 1954, a rebellion broke out simultaneously in the Aurès, in the region of Algiers, and in the department of Oran.

Reports indicate the death of five soldiers, two in Batna and three in Kenchela, of two police officers in Dra-el-Mizan (seventy-five miles from Algiers), and of the son of a *colon* near Cassaigne, while on the road from Arris to Biskra, a young instructor and a *caïd* were mortally wounded. In all, ten deaths—the first of a war still going on and whose victims can no longer be counted.

On the whole, one can see that the Algeria of 1954 —the great mass of Moslems and the *colons*—knew

almost nothing of the little group of men who had
just taken up arms.

Observers on all sides had long known "something
was wrong"; but these same observers did not immediately recognize, in the flare-ups of November 1954, the
great conflagration that gave them nightmares.

From December 1954 to April 1955, I stayed in the
Aurès, the first center of the rebellion, where I had
old peasant friends belonging to all tribes. In private
conversations and in low tones, they told me, speaking
of the men of the underground: "People wonder what
they want."

At the time, the heads of families who constituted
the *jemaas* occasionally revealed their irritation with
those whom everyone then called *imounafqen* (out-
laws), and from the first day the unexpected murder
of a popular young schoolteacher had scandalized
Moslem public opinion, which on this point reacted
in unison with the Europeans (one of the first efforts
of the *imounafqen* propaganda during the months that
followed was to dissociate themselves from this murder).

In the same places, less than six months later, the
word *imounafqen* was no longer used and the current
term for the rebels had become *Hodjadj* (plural of the
word *Hadj*, the title for a Believer who has made the
pilgrimage to Mecca). It appears that the use of this

word was originally intended to deceive any indiscreet listener, but gradually, as in all such cases, the clandestine appellation became so familiar that it became the usual one. It occasionally alternated with locutions such as *yan-negh* (one of ours), *yay-nbarra* (outsiders), *yay-n-oudhrer* (the ones from the mountain).

In Kabylia, where the word *imounafqen* has the same meaning as in the Aurès, it has never, to my knowledge, been used to refer to the men of the underground. At first the Kabyls called *moudjahidin*[1] (fighters for the faith) those who in France were called *fellaga*.[2] Later, even more often than *moudjahidin*, the Kabyls said *yen-nit* (the others) in speaking of them.

During the summer of 1955, the secret organization that had launched the rebellion (the C.R.U.A.— Comité Révolutionnaire d'Unité et d'Action) defined the structures of its two elements: The F.L.N. (Front de Libération Nationale), a political instrument, was to be the synthesis of all the Algerian nationalist movements. The A.L.N. (Armée de Libération Nationale) was to organize the underground.

At this date the people still confused the M.T.L.D.[3] and the Front, and this confusion was to continue dur-

---

[1] Singular: *moudjahad*.
[2] Singular: *felleg*. Arabic plural: *fellaga*. Chaouia plural: *ifellagen*. The French newspapers have long employed the spelling *fellagha*, which is incorrect.
[3] The M.T.L.D. took no part in the elaboration of the 1954

ing the campaigns until the beginning of 1956. The police echoed this ignorance and attempted to destroy everything that looked like an organization—the more innocent the organization, the more vulnerable. This was playing right into the hands of the real clandestine movements.

Two terrorisms face to face

Before February 6, 1956, the machinery of the Algerian revolution was quite insignificant and little known to the Moslem masses. The feelings it inspired in them were vague approval, vague anxiety, and great curiosity.

The electoral campaign of December 1955 and the electoral success of M. Pierre Mendès-France and M. Guy Mollet provoked a timid interest among the Moslem Algerians and a noisy disapproval among the Europeans. The total and immediate capitulation of the President of the Council upon his arrival in Algeria, and the spectacular character of the violent demonstrations that preceded it, inspired, conversely, a profound anxiety among the Moslems, while the Europeans, having grown aware of their power, now aspired to wield it.

It happened that the first major F.L.N. cell was

---

rebellion, and its partisans are at present in violent opposition to those of the F.L.N.

discovered and destroyed at this time. Thanks to the French press, Moslem public opinion learned—for the first time, and not without satisfaction—the importance of the Front organizations.

Each detail was greedily gleaned, commented on, enlarged, and enlistments in the F.L.N. immediately assumed—by April 1956—the rhythm of a mass movement; on every side people sought contact with the clandestine organization and asked its representatives to accept their contributions.

During this period the counterterrorist organizations, which up to then had not been formed, were feverishly organized, for in Algeria everyone decides what to expect by watching the moves of the rival community—which, of course, further accelerates the offensive zeal of each side.

We must not forget that in this double process metropolitan France bears a heavy responsibility. It drove the Frenchmen of Algeria to despair and gave them a "betrayal complex"—and then it released their aggression with no control, an aggression that was understandable but in no way excusable, and extremely dangerous even to themselves. With culpable weakness, metropolitan France also permitted to be destroyed whatever trust the Moslem Algerians still had in her arbitration, leaving them no means of expression save pure violence.

If I recall these events known to everyone, it is because they are directly responsible for the enormous force the great networks (F.L.N. terrorists, French counterterrorists) assumed, releasing, three months later—time in which to organize—mechanisms that are probably irreversible.

Terrorism, counterterrorism, tortures, clandestine executions, murders, official and exemplary executions —in this double system of interlocking chain reactions, we shall first analyze the role of executions, which was decisive.

Executions and attacks (June 1956)

It was madness to let such a war begin. Madder still —and odious—not to call it by its name and not to treat as soldiers the men who were fighting us. "Subversive war" is not a new phenomenon in human history, and our race's instinct for survival has caused it to invent an antidote long ago; the antidote is called honor.

In this kind of war, where neither barbwire nor Maginot Line separates the combatants, but where terrified populations are both the battlefield and its stake, we must either deny the "human nation," that Nation of nations—which is madness and crime—or else unswervingly follow an age-old path so deeply cut into the war-scarred plain of human history that it remains visible at all times and in all places. Loyalty to one's word, respect for one's guest, that solicitude for others known as politeness, a disinterested protection of the weak—all this constitutes a language which is understood on every continent.

To deal with men and not believe in their humanity (in other words, in their reason) is a wicked position, and a stupid one, for it excludes the possibility of an agreement—and there is nothing more dangerous than to drive a whole people to desperation.

For twenty months, the Paris authorities, relying both on our institutions and on a legitimate reluctance, managed to prevent executions. Then, as usual, they yielded and two executions occurred in Algiers.[4]

An execution is in itself ignoble enough to revolt any normal individual having occasion to know at first hand the circumstances that accompany it. The least one can demand to justify these barbarous rites is that they be invoked only to punish some odious, inexcusable crime that is universally condemned and whose author has been identified with certainty.

In the political circumstances of 1956, and in view of a Moslem unanimity that had taken shape by then, the executions were, moreover, affronts which compromise not an irresponsible subordinate (like the tortures), but the entire institutional body. And this is

---

[4] Ferradj and Zabanah (the name was spelled incorrectly on the official record as Zahana).

what a certain stratum of "colonial" public opinion
insisted on, the definitive compromise of the only
possible arbiter of the conflict, in order to render that
conflict insoluble.

Out of political cowardice, intellectual laziness, disintegration of a sense of responsibility, the arbiter let
itself be persuaded.

If, in November 1954, the French police had found
and sentenced the murderer of the schoolteacher Mon-
nerot, it is possible—but not certain—that Moslem
public opinion might have been divided. Eighteen
months later, it was *unanimous* against our justice.

The day after the first two executions, in Algiers
alone there were some thirty attacks with revolvers,
the first ones. They resulted in forty-seven dead or
wounded Europeans.

At the same time, "death commandos" were recruited—whom the people call *fiddayin*,[5] but even
more often *moussebbilin*, the "sacrificed." [6]

Two of the aggressors were shot down, one of whom,

---

[5] Plural of the Arab word *fedday*, "he who purifies."
[6] In Kabyl, *insebbelen* (singular: *insebbel*), from the Arabic
es-sabbil, "the road." Literally, "those whom the caravan
abandons on the road." In its present sense this word was used
for the first time, to my knowledge, in Kabylia, in 1872, to
designate the men who left to scale the walls of Fort-National.

The *insebbelen* are dressed in new clothes, like the dead,
and the prayer of the Absent One is spoken over them. Before
the ceremony, they go to the baths and perfume themselves to
be ready to appear before God.

named Achour, lived at 3 rue de Thèbes; another, taken alive, was executed subsequently. Innumerable arrests then took place in the circles to which the known or presumed terrorists belonged.

Before this date, one could cite cases of tortures in Algeria—there is, moreover, no country in the world completely free from this horrible practice—but they remained isolated. After the first terrorist attacks, torture became the sinister complement of arrest: terrorism justified torture in some people's eyes, while torture and capital punishment, in other people's eyes, made the most murderous attacks permissible.

The first French bomb (July 1956)

The first plastic bomb that exploded in Algeria was a *counterterrorist* bomb—a French bomb. It was responsible for fifty-three deaths (thirty-seven, according to other sources) and innumerable wounded. It demolished several buildings and, according to the municipal report, 280 people found themselves without a roof over their heads (end of July 1956).

The authors of the crime placed the device in position a few minutes before the curfew, in order to claim the greatest possible number of victims, and as it happened, they were mostly women, children, and old men. The choice of victims may have been an accident, but there was nothing accidental about the placement of the bomb itself—at 3 rue de Thèbes—the residence of one of the *moussebbilin* who had been caught trying to avenge Zabanah and Ferradj three months before.

There was no reaction from European public opinion; the papers mentioned the attack without speaking of the number of victims, and the matter was dropped. The newspaper before me as I write devotes nine lines to the incident, repeating the official version: "It is thought that the incident figures in the struggle between members of the F.L.N. and the Messalists."

As a matter of fact, no one in Algiers thought any such thing, for the bomb that had just exploded was a plasticine bomb, and the European population, in July 1956, was far from supposing that either the F.L.N or the Messalists could ever possess such a bomb. Had the police identified the guilty? I don't know. In any case, there was no arrest.

However, suspects were quickly named in many Algerian circles. One Michel Féchoz, along with the celebrated Kovacs,[7] appeared to have led the organiza-

---

[7] Dr. René Kovacs, accused of having committed, in January 1957, an attack against General Salan, commander in chief in Algeria, and of having on this occasion killed Commandant Rodier, was judged with his accomplices by the military tribunal in Paris. To the astonishment of French and foreign public opinion, all the accused were given provisional liberty, and of course the most compromised among them fled. Two years later, during the "barricades" trial, the principals ac-

tion that had manufactured and planted the bomb; their collaborator was presumed to be a D.S.T. (Division de Sécurité Territoriale) inspector named Mestre —who was murdered two months later (September 1956) by one Ahad, who also lived in the rue de Thèbes, in one of the houses adjoining the ruined block. Ahad was condemned to death and executed in June 1957, but he had avenged the innocent dead —his own family—who had been ignored by official justice.

Confronted with an apparently total indifference on the part of French public opinion and French justice, the Moslems were stunned; thereafter they felt they had been delivered—without defense, without arms, without legal recourse of any kind—to murder pure and simple. When, two months later, the first F.L.N. bombs exploded in their turn, they were greeted with exultation by increasingly important sectors of Moslem public opinion, and the planters of the bombs were, of course, to figure as "protectors of the people" and national heroes.

Now, whatever the political party to which he belongs, what Frenchman dares say publicly that an innocent Algerian life taken by a French hand must not be paid for at the same price as an innocent French life taken by an Algerian hand?

---

cused of the insurrection of January 24, 1960, also provisionally freed, escaped under the same conditions.

Yet for six years the severity of our laws weighed in full measure in every case upon one group, and *never* on the other, and this, one must say, despite the efforts of outraged officers and magistrates.

After 1959 some legal sanctions could be taken against Frenchmen responsible for crimes in Algeria, and they somewhat diminished the number of such crimes—but only *somewhat*, no doubt because they were neither numerous nor public enough.

There are crimes and crimes—crimes of temperament, crimes of situation. In this war, more than in any other, the easy, stupid, and cowardly solution was the gradual acceptance of atrocities. And, of course, we fell into it.

The problem was to stop, and to remember that those dragged into the abyss were "men like the others." One dreams of a justice pitiless to the crime and pitying to the criminal. But even before punishing, one must call the crime by its name.

The first F.L.N. bombs (September 30, 1956)

On September 30, 1956, the first F.L.N. bombs exploded in Algiers; two of them claimed numerous victims, for they were planted Sunday afternoon in two of the most popular cafés in the city, the Milk-bar and the Cafétéria. Together they claimed one dead victim and fifty-two wounded. As was the case with the bomb in the rue de Thèbes, a watchful and calculating hatred inspired the choice of the deadliest hour.

This time, on the other hand, the reaction in European circles was tremendous: it filled all the papers for several days and demanded details about the investigation. But that was not all: it also demanded the guilty, and at any price. It demanded them so imperiously that the police, the Army, and the press—which, moreover, vibrated in unison—strove to discover them at any price.

Despite the F.L.N tracts that claimed responsibility for the attack, public opinion and the police first attributed the September 30 explosions to a Communist organization.[8] Why? Simply, no doubt, because it was

---

[8] Members of the Algerian Communist party collaborated with the F.L.N., but the Front agreed to accept them only as individuals, and when they were arrested, French Communists were reluctant about giving them their official support. (Naturally, within the Communist party itself, there was no unanimous opinion on this matter.)

A Frenchman of Algeria and a convinced Communist, Yveton, in order to associate himself completely with the Algerian revolution, planted a bomb in a public building, but took care to hurt no one, and indeed only material damage was caused. He was arrested in the frenzied atmosphere of Algiers, sentenced to capital punishment, and executed.

Abandoned by everyone (including the majority of the French Communist party), in solidarity with the condemned Moslems sharing his cell he recited Moslem prayers with them and it was to the cry of "*Allah Akbar*" (God is great) that he walked to the scaffold.

Men who were condemned to death neither could nor

a job well done and because European public opinion
in Algiers had not yet managed to rid itself, experience
to the contrary, of its stupid customary prejudices concerning "Arab work"; the Army, as yet ill adapted to
Algeria, transposed to Africa its bitter Asian experience
and invented communism where there was none, in
order to be able to combat it.

Leafing through the Algerian newspapers of this
period, we can observe with alarm the collective hysteria that swept away our unfortunate compatriots.
But corresponding to it, in the shadow of the Casbah,
an at least equal hysteria—just as murderous, just as
pathetic—roused the Moslem masses after the July
1956 explosion in the rue de Thèbes; it was reactivated
almost every day by the murders and tortures then carried out, more and more openly, in the city of Algiers.

After May 1957, Moslem children showed their de-
light when an ambulance passed; at the time of the
"lamppost" attacks—which were particularly murderous and claimed random innocent pedestrians as their
victims—the admiration these inspired was public and
general in all non-European neighborhoods. Exactly
two years before, when a French schoolteacher had

---

would sleep before the time when the executioners came for
their victims (between two and three). All the other prisoners, men and women, would be awake too. At three, the whole
prison would echo to the prayer for the condemned, and then
everyone knew there would be no execution that night, which
was the signal to go to sleep.

been mortally wounded in the Aurès, I had personally been able to verify the general horror that this crime had provoked in the most diverse Moslem Algerian circles. When one considers the contrast between this attitude and the joy that was to explode openly after May 1957 in the civil prison of Algiers, in the Casbah, and in every shanty town after a successful attack, one realizes with horror the distance covered in twenty-four months.

We may not say, because of this, that the Algerians are cruel; I have seen the same hideous joy among certain Frenchmen before the grief and suffering of the adversary.

I have also seen—fortunately—innumerable examples of human compassion on both sides. This compassion belongs exclusively to no nation, to no party. One young underground fighter, whose whole family I know well, owes his life to an old police officer of the D.S.T. who saved him out of pure kindness; another was snatched from death by an *ultra*; I know the names of *paras* who spent all their pay to nurse and feed the miserable prisoners they were supposed to guard.

On the other side, F.L.N. political leaders decided to give rewards to their soldiers for taking prisoners—in order to limit somewhat the terrible civil-war practice of killing a disarmed enemy.

There is no such thing as "good civilians" and "bad soldiers"—or the opposite; nor "good Algerians" and "bad F.N.L. fighters"—or the opposite. There are good men and bad men, and situations in which, furthermore, all fools are bad. Unfortunately, fools are legion.

The first conspiracy (May 13, 1956)

By the last three months of 1956, the people who followed Algerian events attentively knew that the French government was no longer being obeyed.

On January 7, 1957, the state's resignation was made official—a grave move for which M. Lacoste will one day be held to account.

The years 1957 and 1958 were terrible ones, when insubordination was displayed in broad daylight, where the most dreadful excesses were unleashed everywhere.

The civil and military organizations that fomented the riots began to exert, at the end of 1956, increasingly strong pressure on the government leaders, constantly threatening to set off the rebellion. Everyone knew that rebellion was imminent; to avoid it, Paris yielded. This was the best way of collaborating with it, for each concession reinforced subversion both technically and morally.

It would take too long to analyze this maceration of justice, of the state, of authority; a single example will be enough to explain this tragic game of "Winner Loses":

In the name of public order (to avoid a popular movement that would be supported by the Army and turned against the French Republic), Algiers demanded executions[9] and obtained in particular that of the student Abderrahmane Taleb. The greatest French names intervened in vain to obtain his pardon, and the student was executed.

In reprisal, the F.L.N. shot three young soldiers they were holding prisoner.

To avenge them, the Algerian populace rushed toward the Casbah, where barrels of gasoline had been

---

[9] Another argument advanced by the Algiers civil and military authorities to support executions was the impossibility of sanctioning the summary executions and kidnappings: "*We arrest criminals,*" they said, "*we hand them over to the regular courts, and these courts pardon them. . . . As long as this goes on, our men will carry out their own verdicts.*"

As a matter of fact, at this horrible price no one was saved, and the future only compromised.

On January 11, 1958 (according to Le Monde), there were 633 death sentences rendered in Algeria, 104 executions, and 165 commuted sentences. There remained 265 condemned men in the process of pardon or execution.

The rate of death sentences was from twenty to thirty a month.

When General de Gaulle became President of the Republic, he commuted all death sentences.

made ready several months before,[1] with the avowed
intention of burning the Arab quarter.

Headed off in time by skillful military strategists,
our French segregationists contented themselves with
pillaging and destroying the seat of the Algerian min-
istry and overturning our government—thereby offend-
ing, with a certain justice, the servile instruments of
their own domination. A little later, delighted with
themselves, they converged on the Forum, kissing the
housemaids of Bab-el-Oued and carrying the little
Arab shoeshine boys in triumph.

The mob, like the bull in the arena, throws itself in
rage on the blood-colored rag the matador brandishes
under its nose. From the matador, we expect tactics
less simple.

For several weeks, a ministerial crisis had disorgan-
ized the nation. The anxious, irritated French public
understood the secret mechanisms that manipulated
the curious parlimentary ballet as little as foreign spec-
tators, for one could see—inexplicably—each party in
turn disavow or abandon its own candidates, or at least
those who, having provoked the crisis, were thereby
qualified to remain or become ministers. The M.R.P.
openly maneuvered against one of its stars, M. Bi-

---

[1] At Froger's burial, a little over a year before, a gasoline sup-
ply truck had followed the procession, ready to have its cargo
poured over the Casbah (which had more than 80,000 in-

dault;[2] the Socialists turned against M. Lacoste, the Radicals against M. Morice.

For everything I have just said in these pages was known to the French politicians who, since November 1, 1954, succeeded one another at the head of the country; *all* attempted to escape from the trap this Algerian war represented for France—it is a diabolic trap, but one understands nothing of its whole horror so long as one has not examined each of its mechanisms.

The Algerian trap

The common tendency is to compare the Algerian situation with that of Morocco or Tunisia, because, like Morocco and Tunisia, Algeria is one of the nations of Islam and, like these two nations, it must deal with French minorities. But Morocco and Tunisia have always maintained an educational system, a state, and a government, while in Algeria these vital nerves that animate a social body had become "colonial"—that is, not only distinct but precisely the contrary. Between Rabat and Paris, between Tunis and Paris, it was enough to loosen a taut cord to restore to each of the

habitants and occupied an area of about a half square mile).
[2] M. Bidault shortly thereafter left the M.R.P. and associated himself with M. Morice to create a short-lived party whose name I have forgotten.

protagonists the ease of movement their vitality required. By loosening the cord between Algiers and
Paris which the French government held at one end,
by increasing the freedom of the public services in the
distant province, the subjection and the dispossession
of the Algerian majority could only be augmented.
This explains why, in Algeria, the first modern nationalists wanted to be Gallicized, not Arabized—and why
they then collided with those who already possessed
French citizenship.

The latter came in part from Spain, Italy, and Malta
and often had no direct or familial tie with French
territory. Like all who claim a contested possession,
they exhibited a blind, desperate passion in refusing
rights equivalent to their own to that Algerian population which, for four or five generations, had shared
our lot on every battlefield. Once again: the Europeans of Algeria were French because they wanted to
be French (and their children are French, without
argument), but they did not have to interpose themselves between the Algerians and France, as they did,
to their misfortune.

These French circles of North Africa are normally
tumultuous, but during the time when they served as
experimental terrain for the military "psychologists" [3]

---

[3] Members of the S.A.S. (Section Administrative Specialisé),
the "psychological service" of the French Army. Its specialty
was "brainwashing." *Tr. note.*

(January 1957 to January 1961), frenzy reached the pitch of delirium—a hysteria inconceivable to those who did not have the opportunity to measure its effects, a hysteria that few nerves could resist.

Seeing Frenchmen leave for Algeria who boasted of being "anti-*ultra*" and seeing them again, shortly afterward, more "segregationist" than our worst hysterics in Algiers or Oran, I often thought of a charming old lady, a friend of my family's; her case is not unique, for I have subsequently heard other stories almost identical to hers.

A descendant of the poor, strict Vendée nobility, brought up in an extremely religious boarding school, she married an Englishman, also a Catholic, and as a bride of twenty accompanied her husband to India, somewhere between Guntur and Vijayawada. After five or six years there, she realized one day that she believed in metempsychosis and, alarmed, immediately confessed the fact to an extremely old priest who had lived in India for over half a century. The priest, perhaps believing the same thing himself, gave her absolution without comment. Several years passed; she became a widow, settled her affairs, and returned to end her days in the village of her birth. Here, too, she confessed her beliefs, but the curé of her parish, flabbergasted by this strange sin that was unknown to the peasantry of the Basse-Loire, absolved her by a hairbreadth. Two or three years more passed, and one fine morning she was delighted to discover that she no longer believed in metempsychosis. Happy ending.

For many years, officials and officers, specially sifted to resist the sirens of Algiers, have been sent there by our governments. They yield much sooner than the young bride from Poitou.

The more diligent they are, the more complete and swift their mental capitulation. I have known mild and silent men whom the four hours in the plane were enough to transform into crude fanatics; on the way back to Paris, they recover their habitual civility no less swiftly.

Among our military leaders, many were well-meaning, but the Army, powerfully established on the southern shore of the Mediterranean and furnished, moreover, with its "psychological service," quickly formed an autonomous society and undertook to make the inhabitants of Algeria see the devil in broad daylight. With the French, the success was brilliant: like two parallel mirrors, French civilians and soldiers "intoxicated" each other to an extreme degree. On the other hand, the warm rain of propaganda slid off the Moslems as though off a duck's back.

In the name of this French minority that is so dangerous and so exposed—dangerous because exposed, exposed because dangerous—after January 1957 we found three elements combining: organized networks not flinching before crime itself; pressure groups possessing funds and high-placed complicities; and last, a pathetic mass of workers, the mobs of Algiers and Oran, genuinely terrified by the F.L.N. attacks and by the threat of being handed over defenseless to an enemy who, they were well aware, had serious reasons for revenge.

This conjunction represented, for four years, a permanent temptation for our enthusiasts of *coups d'état*, for it seemed possible to modulate the revolution as one plays the piano, with the fingertips, and— until they pressed the detonator at the right moment— the fear the detonation inspired could be exploited quite fruitfully in Paris. As for the poor *pieds noirs*, they were the unconscious tool of these slippery characters.

At the end of 1956, informed people knew that the probabilities of a civil war were increasing from day to day and that when it came to open fighting, the enormous French Army stationed in North Africa would have the last word. In the final analysis, the arbiter of France would be the highest-ranking general in Algeria.

In this light the attack against General Salan, his almost contrite attitude after having had the luck to escape his assassins, his confusion when the firecracker of May 13 exploded under his nose, assume their full meaning.

For several weeks, in Paris, the deputies of all parties, at last realizing the danger and much more aware of their duty than their electors suppose, tried, through the ballet steps of the parliamentary procedure, to lead toward power a man worthy of wielding it. It was the choice of this man which apparently unleashed the riot.

M. Pflimlin, a patriotic Alsatian, appeared to have nothing about him to disturb our frenetic Algerian nationalists, but his reputation for being an upright, honest, uncompromising man, on the other hand, quite justly alarmed officials and soldiers somewhat too advanced in the labyrinths of an illegality that had hitherto more or less covered the men in power. This, I believe, was the match that set off the infernal machine. Prematurely, luckily for us.

In the brawl that followed, only one man, who was able to rally elements scattered to the four corners of our political horizon, had any chance of keeping France from breaking in two.

A month before, General de Gaulle numbered very few advocates in the Chamber, and rather few in the Army, but to each of these groups he seemed more acceptable than the other's choice. Between the two, the distressed French people coagulated around this name and thereby forced its military wing and its parliamentary wing to make the best of a bad job.

In the first referendum (September 28, 1958) the General had 17,666,828 supporters and 4,624,475 opponents.[4]

When one questions people belonging to this very small minority, one discovers that it was composed of electors resolutely advocating parliamentarianism, determined communists, and crypto-fascist *cagoulards*—three unreconcilable blocs, each of which can suddenly be enlarged if the occasion allows. (The last seems, in France, the least consistent, though one must add to it a few irreducible supporters of Marshal Pétain.)

Fraternization

During this period another operation was taking place in Algiers—the various instances of fraternization. The work of military elements (but, contrary to what one might expect, not the work of the so-called psychological service, which instead was almost its only victim), fraternization had the unexpected merit of sweeping the European crowd, even its extremist elements, into spectacular *rapprochements*. It failed, on the other hand, among the Moslems, who, after General Massu's success in Algiers, were inaccessible to our warbling.

While embracing in the Forum the people whom

---

[4] 20.75 per cent.

they had literally wanted to burn a few hours earlier,[5]
our fanatic *ultras* rallied with enthusiasm to the policy
of integration they had hitherto rejected so bitterly.
This policy, once strongly advocated by Moslem intellectuals, could be used against the policy of independence, the watchword of the F.L.N.—at least this was
the intention of the artists who were orchestrating the
score. As for the choristers, there is every reason to suppose that they were not so subtle, and were actually
embracing in good faith.[6]

Thus most *engagé* military elements understood
that these embraces would not stop the war, that
peace would come through the extremes—that is, the

---

[5] Meanwhile, they had relaxed by despoiling the seat of the
Government-General, thereby overturning, they believed, the
French Republic.
[6] At each burial of a terrorist victim, the French mobs in Algiers assaulted passing Moslems. In certain circumstances, the
forces of law and order intervened, but not always, and notably not during the year 1957. During these crises of hysteria,
men were killed and wounded, and Moslem shops pillaged.
Severely reprimanded by their curé the day after one of these
attacks, the parishioners of Bab-el-Oued, crestfallen, returned
what they had stolen. Unfortunately, the dead cannot be
brought back to life.
Since May 13, 1958, at least in the big cities, the French
crowds, accepting the fiction that "the Moslems are with us,"
have stopped making any Algerian responsible for any attack.
Even while the unfortunate victims are being buried, the Moslem populace continues to go about its affairs without anxiety
—at least since 1959.

combatants of both armies—and that the "third force" was a pure chimera. But they had virtually no means of making themselves heard, and their attempts at analysis were diluted by the absurd rationalizations of the psychological service, the "second bureau."

As a matter of fact, after 1957 the F.L.N. was too closely associated with the Algerian masses for any lasting *détente* to occur without its total agreement. Besides, the French leaders who suddenly began advocating integration and fraternization were well known to the wretched Moslem population, which mistrusted them altogether. The *coup de grâce* was the benediction of *L'Echo d'Alger*, a paper which the Moslem Algerians, for many years, have always read attentively to know the opposite of what they should be thinking.

May 13, 1958, was nevertheless, in Algeria, the signal for a truce, unfortunately a short one, for because of a misunderstanding French civilians and soldiers had convinced themselves that all Algerians were anti-F.L.N. and therefore should be treated "as Frenchmen." The Moslems, delighted by the change, and supposing, moreover, that General de Gaulle would attempt to create a true peace—that is, an agreement with the real Algeria—appreciated the *détente*.

Like all misunderstandings, this one was short-lived. The military police soon realized that the F.L.N. had lost none of its advantages, and since the Army retained General Salan, certain of his elements were free to begin demolishing, in a few hours, all the fragile "pacifications" which another part of the Army, with great difficulty and several years of work, had managed to impose.

All this amply explains the failure of fraternization in Moslem circles.

On the other hand, many soldiers and some French civilians, delighted by the public embraces and the carnival in the Forum, clung to their nostalgia for it a long time.

To a certain degree these instances of unilateral fraternization marked a stage, all the same, helping to wear down the racism of our "segregationists."

Moreover, there is a great deal to say about this strange racism, which is so different from that of the Anglo-Saxon peoples and which, in many aspects, is more suggestive of a class struggle.

For instance, in all the big hotels and restaurants of Algiers and Oran, the two populations have always coexisted, and since the economic advance in some Moslem circles, Moslems occupy the same apartments, live in the same neighborhoods, and frequent the same merchants as the ex-*colons*.

As a proof of Algerian racism, certain sport clubs are often cited, where, before and after 1953, the young *ultras* attempted to keep to themselves, giving as the excuse for their ostracism: "The —— don't want to let us get a look at their wives' noses, so why should

we let them see the asses on ours?" We are also told
of the *apartheid* of some of the wives of policemen
and customs officers who refused to associate with one
of their compatriots who had married a Moslem.

All this collapses at an incredible speed and, contrary to what most people suppose, the war contributes
to this collapse.

Of course it feeds hatred, fear, and bitterness, but
it also emphasizes mixtures, and it has annihilated the
technological contempt of our "segregationists" for
"Arab work."

As a logical consequence, mixed marriages, already
extremely numerous before 1954, have grown even
more common.

The second conspiracy (January 24, 1960, and thereafter)

Between the fraternizations of May 1958 and General de Gaulle's declaration concerning self-determination (September 16, 1959), Algeria lived through a
period of unimaginable confusion, during which each
subordinate pursued his own policy—and with a high
hand.

Algiers lived through an oscillating hysteria in which
one or the other community alternately triumphed
while the other gave itself up to despair.

Between September 16, 1959, and the unsuccessful

coup of January 24, 1960—that is, during the last
quarter of 1959—the tension in Algiers became unen-
durable, and it was easy, once again, to claim that the
least shock would set off the charge from one moment
to the next. As a matter of fact, shocks are a daily
affair, at least in this city.

Afterward, some of us romantically imagined that
malicious diplomats sent to the general in command
of the Algiers sector that journalist whose article
launched a classic and familiar process: a soldier's public declaration; the usual sanction taken against him;
protests of third parties against this sanction.

An inverse hypothesis seems just as plausible, for
many officials and soldiers remained loyal to the President of the Republic while deploring most of his
actions. They may have sought occasions to "open
General de Gaulle's eyes," to "clarify their own responsibility," without realizing, no doubt, the em-
barrassment they caused those who benefited from
their own blindness.

The removal of General Massu could embarrass fac-
tious elements—as did the appointment of M. Pflimlin
eighteen months before. In short, Massu's departure
was the signal for an insurrection that appeared to be
badly prepared, since it collapsed. The French mob
assassinated 14 policemen and wounded 136.

Before January 24, 1960, a civil administration in
which the younger elements were predominant had

regained certain positions so inopportunely conceded
to the Army three years before. Great efforts were
made in these areas, and they were not all ineffective
—but even before 1954, Algeria was a sick country,
and its situation after six years of a terrible war dis-
courages even the most optimistic.

Among the difficult undertakings, we must mention
the series of elections during which blameless officials
attempted to stop the falsifications; we may note,
thanks to their efforts, slight progress from one series
to the other.

People cognizant of North African affairs were
nevertheless unanimously hostile to these attempts,
which risked extending the war by creating a pseudo-
Parliament. The insistence of the French government
is explained, apparently, by other motives: to familiar-
ize the rural populations with the features of democracy, to fill—however summarily, however provisionally
—this dangerous void, the caverns yawning in the Algerian lungs after not only six years of war and a series
of fixed elections but 130 years of colonization, during
which a foreign population had infiltrated into every
vein of this country and controlled electorally its vital
centers.

Despite these arguments, whose weight is real, I remained hostile to these elections because they created
a momentary obstacle to peace, because this delay
seemed to me of enormous consequence and insuffi-

ciently counterbalanced by its advantages. So long as
the war lasted, we could expect nothing of Algerian
democracy, which remained "a body in the under-
taker's hands."

In France, De Gaulle's speech of September 16,
1959, was received with relief: "Since we have no need
to fight any more, we won't fight any more, or at least
not for long." This was the notion of many Frenchmen, who were grateful to General de Gaulle for being
the man to rid them of this ordeal. But a year later
we were still fighting, understanding less and less why
we were still bothering to oblige Algeria to do what
she wanted to do anyway (particularly since everyone
knew she would finally want what the F.L.N. prescribed for her). People can accept their sacrifices if
they understand why they are making them. After all,
life is something precious.

The same thing could be said about the Algerians.
Why were they fighting if they had obtained in advance what they asked for? One can even say that the
deadlier the battles were for them[7] and the heavier the
ordeals of their civilians, starting from the moment
this war ceased to have a purpose, the less reason they
had to prolong it.

---

[7] The French population is five times more numerous than
the Algerian population, and our official losses in human lives
do not number a tenth of those of the Algerian underground.
As for the sufferings of the Algerian civilian population, they
have been unspeakable.

Yet in the agony of Moslem Algeria, the promises of September 16, 1959, did not awaken the least gleam of hope—words, phrases, which everyday reality contradicted at each moment. It was only four months later—January 24, 1960—that the Algerians, during the rebellion of their oppressors, glimpsed the value of these promises. And it was when they saw the firmness of the Paris government in dealing with the riot that they decided their almost instinctive confidence of May 1958 was justified, that the misery crouching over their nation like an enormous beast could be driven off.

The same phenomenon occurred after General de Gaulle's speech of November 4, 1960. It was scarcely listened to by a discouraged people. But the outraged reactions it provoked from the French *ultras* in the days that followed awakened, after the fact, the attention of the Algerians, and people who had refused to listen to the speech began reading what De Gaulle had said.

Meanwhile the Melun talks had occurred. In Algeria, they had aroused great hopes, and even in Tunis, where the Algerians were supposed to be completely F.L.N.-ized, their emotion, their joy at seeing this nightmare end overflowed publicly.

Yet these meetings, preliminary as they were, and having no other object than to settle the details of an eventual encounter, failed.

It is true that the delegates, mandated by the ministers we pretended to ignore, took one of the regular planes from Tunis to Paris, got out at Orly, and proceeded to some suitable villa, where they met the officials duly invested by the French government—after which the thunder didn't thunder, the Forum of Algiers didn't move, and there was not even an errand boy to be found for a hostile demonstration. The world concluded that the French government was making itself obeyed in France, which in itself constituted a welcome event—particularly welcome, it must be admitted, because many Frenchmen counted on this new authority to free them from the calamitous *expédition d'Alger*. Now, far from being freed from it, they felt the war weighing still more heavily on their shoulders, on account of this hope momentarily glimpsed and immediately dispelled.

Their disappointment was as nothing beside that of the Algerian population. When they discovered the blind alley into which for so many years this nation, which circumstances have brought so close to us and made so intelligible, had groped its way, even mere onlookers were filled with despair.

Abroad, however, the people who took the trouble to keep informed had long known that Algeria would —certainly and soon—be independent. And perhaps allied with our country, *if we consented to this, and if Algeria consented too*. They know this the way people know that the sea is salty and that ice is cold.

These same people also know that no nation in the world except France can provide for the Algerians the 800,000 industrial jobs of which they have a vital and immediate need—while, alone on earth, Frenchmen and Algerians seem to be unaware of the fact that they must understand one another and that, by not doing so, each is asphyxiating his own country.

Separated like two elements

The war, following inflexible laws, though every day intensifying the practical mixture of the two populations and their anxious curiosity about each other, has seemed to divide them further and further. Between them stretches the smooth, fragile, but continually renewed partition that isolates two elements: air, water—autonomous universes.

Nothing was more alarming than to listen to the echoes of two worlds so close and so distinct, and to lean over mute Algeria, when the chatter of fraternization still vibrated in our memory.

Listening to the Moslem Algerians of any faction— the French sympathizers, the prisoners arrested for nothing, the prisoners arrested for something, the high officials of our administration, those whom France has stripped of everything, those who owe everything to France, those who are afraid of the

F.L.N., those who are afraid of our police—it was all the same, when they dared speak.

Not one among them, in the cities or in the country, who doesn't number in his immediate family at least one victim of our repression. And none who hasn't some relative engaged in the rebellion and at least one seriously compromised in the eyes of the F.L.N. May fate spare them a purge from either side, for not one family will escape without losses!

In a Kabyl village, an F.L.N. representative is betrayed to the French soldiers by an enemy of his family. Ambushed, caught, mistreated, he agrees to turn *harki*.[8] Now he is free, with good pay and rifle.

A few weeks later he murders the man who had turned him in when he had been a *felleg*. No investigation of this murder. (What is one more dead man in Algeria?) And since the murderer is a *harki*, the victim was necessarily suspect.

Now the dead man's family watches the *harki's* comings and goings. When they kill him (and they will certainly kill him), will they have killed a member of the F.L.N. or an enemy of the F.L.N.?

I know the names of the two families in question, and there are thousands of others who live in analogous circumstances or in situations even more confused.

While for six years our society has reacted only to

---

[8] A Moslem Algerian fighting on the French side.

the crimes attributed—whether rightly or wrongly—
to our adversaries (ignoring or wanting to ignore our
own), among nine million Moslems the converse has
occurred: here the echo of our exactions—true or false
—spread (and spread exclusively) while the noble
deeds attributed to the underground fighters were ex-
cessively amplified.

In the areas where the population is extremely
dense—those which "pacification" has most sorely
tried—when terrorism claimed a victim his family generally tried to conceal or disguise his death—in any
case, to surround it with no ceremony. Did a certain
amount of rallying to our cause occur? In some cases.
But these were sincere and valid only in the areas
where the A.L.N. had committed violences—in other
words, affirmed its presence and won successes. On
the other hand, wherever our troops have won, France
has lost. Such were the rules of this hideous game.

Danger is a fearful amalgamator and always rele-
gates ideas and theories to the background. For the
moment, the Algerian population as a whole stands
together.

Does it approve of the F.L.N. on every point? It
doesn't know, and doesn't care, for it is possessed by an
impassioned solidarity—the brotherhood of combat.

I could cite a thousand examples of this, whether
the Kabyl baker who in 1959 gave away his bread
free, or the town where every Moslem home took in

strangers because a military patrol, one market day, came to arrest every peasant of the region.

This solidarity does not imply a total community of thought (which exists nowhere), but it implies a profound and strong feeling that is the very root of *national* feeling. One can argue the existence or the non-existence of the Algerian nationality at this or that period of history, but after six years of a war like this one, the Algerian nation stands before us. We have forged and tempered it with our own hands.

For how explain the almost instantaneous elimination of the M.N.A. in the regions of dense Moslem population (Kabylia, the big Algerian cities), when its strong and ancient structures maintain it in the zones where this population is scattered (plateaus, steppes, French suburbs)? How justify the empirical observation of our S.A.S. officers that, when a grouping exceeds a thousand persons, it escapes "psychological" control? How account for all this, if not by the fact that as soon as public opinion formed in Algeria, it immediately associated itself with *those who fight.*

Are they, then, all against us? This is what is so strange: no.

A young officer told me at the end of 1959: "You can't say they don't like us. Only they prefer the F.L.N."

Before the collapse of the Melun talks, many observers admitted that 90 per cent of the Moslem population sympathized with the F.L.N.; they added that more than 60 per cent of this same population considered its future to be linked to that of France. There would therefore be some 50 per cent of the Moslem population of Algeria which at that moment was *simultaneously* for the F.L.N. and for maintaining privileged relations with France.

The war for nothing

The war, after General de Gaulle's declaration on self-determination, has gradually lost all its justifications. Henceforth, on both sides, we are fighting for nothing.

All the elite groups of the Maghreb nations have engaged, since adolescence, in a double participation: first, in the structures dreaming of independence and consequently steeped in love, pride, and concern for their country; subsequently (or rather, at the same time), in a complete absorption of French culture, imbibed at the very heart of our universities.

An Indian statesman who visited Algeria at the end of 1957 said to me in a very thoughtful tone: "*All these schools seem on a level with those in France.*" And indeed they are. We have given this nation the worst of what we had, and the best.

Everything said and written about the French of Algeria, on that opaque screen they have stretched for a century between the other Algerians and France, risks giving an unfair and false image of them. They are men like the rest, no worse than the rest. As elsewhere, one finds among them exceptional merit, as much on the level of intelligence as on that of courage and spirit.

When a Frenchman of Algeria understands the Moslems of his country, he understands them better, more fraternally, than many so-called liberal Frenchmen, because his comprehension and his friendship have no theoretical character, because they expose him to dangers, to sufferings, often even to the animosity and mistrust of his own kind. This warm, lucid, steady friendship is then a richer gift than the benevolence of those pacific neutrals who, having never hated, suppose it is easy to overcome hatred.

Even among the most fanatic, the most committed, the most compromised *ultras*, one almost always finds curious ambivalences. They explain certain incredibly rapid reversals, such as those of the fraternizations. They will hold surprises for us in the future.

To understand one civilization properly, one must know at least two—and deeply. Indeed, the genius of childhood sometimes opens both doors at once to those born on the watershed of two impassioned worlds.

This double knowledge, like the vision of our two

eyes, is an indispensable corrective; it offers balance, a sense of perspective, and in a world where all national interests must try more than ever to assume some order, it is the essential virtue of our heads of state.

It is no accident that Moroccan generals and Tunisian diplomats are today among the surest supports of international arbitration; they have studied their "humanities."

In Algeria, this searching and deepening of the national character is not the privilege of only one class, and it can animate a whole future.

But all this exists only in possibility—a possibility called peace. Before peace, one cannot hope to see any public opinion emerging. Peace means negotiations— that is clear to everyone—negotiations of Frenchmen with Algerians, negotiations of Algerians with Frenchmen.

Peace

FOR A LITTLE over six years the Algerians have been fighting for their independence—that is, for a self-determined Algeria. They have it, apparently.

Meanwhile, the men who lead them have changed. Not that they have all died and been replaced by others, but those who survive have in these six years accumulated experiences that make them very different from the Garibaldian patriots who went underground so long ago.

For instance, seven years ago all the Algerian nationalists believed that Algeria was a rich plum that a greedy France was gorging herself on. Today they know that Algeria is very poor, scarcely viable; that it weighs heavy on a France which, in this war, has constantly followed confused, inconsiderate, but disinterested passions.

In 1954, no one spoke of the Saharan oil, and I do not think its existence has in the slightest influenced people like Mostfa ben Boulaïd, Bachir, Chihani,

Belkacem Krim, Mohammed Ben Bella, Mohammed Boudiaf, Rabah Bitat.

The mass of the French people had entered the war without even knowing it, and consequently without asking itself questions; as for its leaders, they had too much to do from day to day to be able to think of the future as well. Those who tried—for instance, Pierre Mendès-France—were automatically eliminated.

After 1956, on the other hand, we heard a great deal about the marvelous profits of the Sahara and its oil, and about the vague "insularity of the franc zone" which that oil would secure.

It is enough, in fact, for any average elector to read any paper to discover that purchasers of oil are fewer than the sellers; that the Saharan oil will be valuable only if we ourselves buy it (and we will have to pay for it, in any case, above the world price—which means that the arrangements will be made without difficulty); that our balance of exchange, with a little care, despite twenty years of uninterrupted war, has readily recovered an equilibrium, without the help of oil. As for our economic autarchy, it is venerable antiquity that was in its prime during the Empire (the First, Josephine's) but which in our time is as archaic as a carriage.

In addition, many people in France believed (as I did) that throughout this horrible and stupid war the life of a little Algerian shepherd was worth more than all the oil to be found in the Sahara.

Concerning the extremely conditional value of the oil, the Algerians are still better informed than we are. The few manipulations to which it has given rise, they have seen from closer range than we have and, I suppose, no longer let themselves be deluded by them.

Our legitimate war goal, our avowed war goal, was the safeguarding of the lives and interests of a considerable population that claimed the name and the protection of France; that is, a million Frenchmen identified as such and a small number of Algerians who have every claim on us they can ask, save one— that of making us begin the Hundred Years' War all over again.

Our second war goal, not avowed but quite legitimate, consisted in not adding to our twenty years of foolish and distant wars twenty more of civil wars—for it is a fact that our army has managed only with a great deal of pain to disabuse itself of the romance of "psychological warfare."

As a matter of fact, fighting a war against one's own army is a prospect that has nothing agreeable about it.

Contrary to what certain intellectuals think, soldiers are no more stupid than they are, and intellectuals have as much patriotism as career officers. The dissension which temporarily separates them comes from the fact that they do not have the same sources of information. Of course, if we could offer an extended world tour to all our subordinates, they would probably understand in considerable numbers to what degree the young "revolutionary war" and the old Machiavellianisms are henceforth perilous and contrary to the permanent interests of France.

Not to disobey is one thing; to obey is another. Now, the status quo in Algeria cannot be maintained; like a plane, our government must move, and move quickly, in order not to fall. For this it needs active obedience from the Army. I imagine that this was the motivation of the January 1961 referendum.

On either side, French and Algerians now live in dreadful tension, and the least *faux pas* may reverse their opinions at any moment.

For the time being, the French want peace, they follow De Gaulle, and they would obviously disavow the formenters of insurrectional difficulties—but a portion of our public opinion would certainly do an about-face if, during the days to come, a great injustice were committed to the detriment of the Frenchmen of Algeria.

In Tunisia and in Morocco, the transition from French control to Tunisian and Moroccan control took place in a few hours without costing the life of a single Frenchman. But Morocco and Tunisia are not Algeria; in Algeria one cannot imagine a safe hiatus of authority after six years of furious war. Yet

"Algerian independence" means "Algerian order."

This transition from one kind of order to another could not be made directly, and it was natural that the French government should seek an intermediary stage. It is no less true, however, that to deal with a transition and also excusable but lamentable susceptibilities would compromise the future of our Algerian compatriots.

The lasting interests of the French population of Algeria were in fact more greatly endangered in a "prefabricated" independent Algeria than in a negotiation with the F.L.N., for in the former likelihood a counterbalance would be missing—that of the Algerian interests in France. As a matter of fact, these considerably offset the weight of French interests in Algeria, and are the best guarantees, the only real guarantees, the French there have.

Conversely, when the Algerian leaders speak of an "internationalization of the conflict," they must realize, of course, that if it were forced upon us it would greatly endanger the Algerian interests in France—which are more *vital* for Algeria than the French interests in Algeria are for France.

One can choose one's friends, but not one's enemies. We are what we are, the Algerians what they are, but it is with us that they will make peace, and with no one else. And we with them, and only with them.

GERMAINE TILLION, specialist on Algerian sociology, is Directeur d'Etudes at L'Ecole Pratique des Hautes Etudes (Sorbonne) (Social Science Department) and teaches the course *Ethnographie du Maghreb*.

Mlle Tillion spent the years from 1934 to 1940 in Algeria on scientific missions. From 1940 to 1942 she was the chief of a Resistance network, and then underwent three years of imprisonment and was condemned to death on five counts. She wrote a history of the Second World War, and since 1954 has made several extensive trips to Algeria in behalf of the French Government.

Germaine Tillion has been awarded the *Rosette d'officier de la Légion d'honneur*, the *Croix de guerre*, and the *Rosette d'officier* for her Resistance work; and her studies of the Algerian people, both anthropological and sociological, have greatly influenced French opinion.

June, 1961